Battle of Britain

Airfields of 11 Group

Peter Jacobs

Pen & Sword
AVIATION

This book is dedicated to Dad, who would have enjoyed reading this book, but sadly won't get the chance.

First published in Great Britain in 2005 by
PEN & SWORD AVIATION
An imprint of
Pen & Sword Books Ltd
47 Church Street
Barnsley
South Yorkshire
S70 2AS

Copyright © Peter Jacobs, 2005

ISBN 1 84415 164 6

The right of Peter Jacobs to be identified as Author of this work has been asserted by him in accordance with the Copyright, Designs and Patents Act 1988.

A CIP catalogue record for this book is available from the British Library

Printed and bound in Great Britain
By CPI UK

Pen & Sword Books Ltd incorporates the Imprints of Pen & Sword Aviation, Pen & Sword Maritime, Pen & Sword Military, Wharncliffe Local history, Pen & Sword Select, Pen & Sword Military Classics and Leo Cooper.

For a complete list of Pen & Sword titles please contact
PEN & SWORD BOOKS LIMITED
47 Church Street, Barnsley, South Yorkshire, S70 2AS, England
E-mail: enquiries@pen-and-sword.co.uk
Website: www.pen-and-sword.co.uk

ACKNOWLEDGEMENTS

This book has been an absolute joy to write. My interest in the Battle of Britain goes all the way back to my childhood, when I was simply in awe of 'the Few'. I could never have imagined that one day I would meet some of those who fought in the battle, something which has been largely due to having served on a number of fighter squadrons during my career in the Royal Air Force.

A book such as this could not have been written without help from many people. One in particular was Pat Wells, who served as a young Hurricane pilot with No. 249 Squadron during the Battle of Britain. I only knew Pat during the last seven years of his life, but even though he lived in South Africa we exchanged many letters and phone calls over the years and I was privileged to meet him during his last two visits to the UK. Indeed, as a family, we were honoured to have Pat with us on 15 September 2000, the sixtieth anniversary of the Battle of Britain. During our friendship Pat was most generous in letting me have numerous photographs and articles, as well as sharing with me his experiences of the Second World War, and in particular the Battle of Britain.

During my time as a staff officer at HQ No. 11 Group at Bentley Priory, I was also privileged to meet several other former Battle of Britain pilots during the annual Battle of Britain cocktail parties and the Fighter Command Association dinners held at Bentley Priory. My thanks go to all those who have helped contribute to my library of photos and personal accounts over the years.

Although I have studied the Battle of Britain over several years, I had not previously toured the airfields. This I found absolutely fascinating. Whilst many have been developed for commercial or civil aviation, or have disappeared altogether, it is still possible at some to sample the atmosphere of what it was like to serve there during the battle. For example, there is still evidence at airfields such as Biggin Hill and Kenley. My visit to the St George's Chapel of Remembrance was particularly moving and my thanks go to the Reverend (Squadron Leader) Andrew Jolly, the Chairman of the Chaplaincy Council at Biggin Hill, and Lawrie Chester, one of the custodians at the Chapel. My chance meeting with Andrew was most welcome, as he had been the station padre during my flying days at RAF Coningsby. Whilst at

Biggin Hill I was also grateful to my friend, Richard Black, for taking me to the site of what is known locally as the 'Leaves Green Dornier'.

I would also like to thank the staff at No. 615 Volunteer Gliding School (VGS) at Kenley, Flight Lieutenant Andy Griffin, who is the Commanding Officer of No. 450 (Kenley) Squadron Air Training Corps, and the locals at the Wattenden Arms. Whilst books offer valuable information, sometimes there is no substitute for local knowledge!

I would also like to thank others for their help and contributions towards this book, in particular, Frank Anderson and members of the Croydon Airport Society, Jack Coppendale of the Tangmere Military Aviation Museum, Alan Couchman at North Weald and both John Bulbeck and Kevin Fellingham at the Martlesham Heath Control Tower Museum. I am also particularly grateful to Peter Turner, the Curator of the Spitfire and Hurricane Memorial Building at Manston, for making me so welcome and spending much of his time sharing his local knowledge of the airfield and its history during the Battle of Britain. I would like to thank David Brocklehurst, the Chairman of the Kent Battle of Britain Museum, for sharing his knowledge of Hawkinge and Lympne. For my visit to the underground bunker at Uxbridge I would like to thank Chris Wren, who not only gave a fascinating guided tour but also gave me the benefit of his knowledge of No. 11 Group during the Battle of Britain. During my visit to the site of the former airfield at Gravesend, I was grateful to Marion Crear at the Cascades Leisure Centre for letting me into the leisure centre early one Sunday morning. There are many other locals who helped me during my visits; I thank them all.

Serving in the RAF, particularly on various fighter squadrons and at Bentley Priory, has given me access to much material over the years, such as squadron diaries, combat reports and photos. However, I could not have produced this book without material from other sources. I would like to thank the staff at the Air Historical Branch, Bentley Priory, in particular my friend Graham Day for helping me with material over the years and my former RAF colleague, Mary Hudson, for help with photographs. I would also like to thank the staff at the RAF Museum, Hendon, the staff at the Imperial War Museum and the staff at the Public Records Office at Kew. Without the help and co-operation of all these people, authors and historians like myself would not be able to pursue our interest. My final thanks go to my old friend Ken Delve who, during one cold and wet day in an office at RAF Finningley, started me on this seemingly never-ending road of writing.

CONTENTS

INTRODUCTION

To historians and aviation enthusiasts alike, the Battle of Britain is special. It was a period when Britain was alone and all that stood in the way of a German invasion was a defence system based on equipment, some advanced technology and, of course, the refusal to accept defeat by those who were part of it. At the forefront of the battle were the squadrons of Fighter Command. As the world looked on, the young men that were to become 'the Few' carried enormous responsibility with them every time they faced the onslaught of the mighty *Luftwaffe*. They carried the hopes and expectations of the nation and the free world.

Although it was Fighter Command that bore the brunt of the battle, it must also be remembered that the other operational commands played their part during the summer of 1940 to deter the threat of a German invasion. Coastal Command flew continuous reconnaissance sorties and patrols, and Bomber Command attacked the Channel ports and other targets supporting the planned invasion of England. Bomber Command even managed a retaliatory attack on Berlin on the night of 25/26 August following the German bombing of London the night before. Of course, the heroics of 'the Few' could not have been possible without the support of 'the Many'. The defence system involved men and women, military and civilian, all doing their bit to ensure that Britain survived. The airfields were a part of that system. In fact, to the RAF's senior commanders, such as Hugh Dowding and Keith Park, they were vital. The Germans, of course, knew that and it is no surprise that they turned their attention to destroying the airfields of Fighter Command, and in particular No. 11 Group, during the height of the battle in August and September 1940.

These airfields were strategically important during that summer. Before Hitler could launch an invasion of Britain, the *Luftwaffe* had to defeat the RAF and it was the young men of No. 11 Group that had to bear the brunt of the battle. The technological breakthrough of radar provided Britain with the vital advantage of an early warning system, which gave Fighter Command precious time to prepare for an attack. However, without the use of so many airfields the RAF could not have been in the right place at the right time, and in sufficient numbers to take on the might of the *Luftwaffe*. In short, had the RAF been defeated in the skies over southern England during the summer of 1940 there was nothing that could have stopped Hitler's plan of invasion.

To Hugh Dowding all the airfields were vital, not only the regular ones of Fighter Command but also those of other commands. There was a plan in place for squadrons to use other airfields if it ever became necessary to evacuate Fighter Command's main bases. Each sector airfield within No. 11 Group had an alternative allocated to it, from which it could operate. For example, Tangmere's alternative was Odiham, an airfield belonging to No. 22 Group. Kenley's nominated alternative was Worthy Down, which was controlled by the Admiralty, and other alternatives included airfields of Bomber and Training Commands. The plan was never put into practice, but, as the Battle of Britain peaked during August and September 1940, No. 11 Group used many different airfields at various times; not all of which belonged to it, or indeed to Fighter Command.

Every airfield that was used operationally by No. 11 Group at some time during the battle is covered in this book in some detail. It soon becomes clear just how many airfields the group used during the battle and just how dispersed the squadrons were. Twenty-seven airfields were used and they were well spread across the south and east: seven in Kent, five in West Sussex, one in Surrey, eight in Greater London, five in Essex and one in Suffolk.

Each airfield has its own history but it is the people who worked there and the events that took place there that makes each one special; all those serving at the airfields contributed towards the overall success. The ground crew worked tirelessly to ensure that the aircraft remained serviceable during the battle. They had to be refuelled and rearmed as quickly as possible after landing to make sure that they were ready to go up again as soon as the call came. The airfield's defences had to be manned and able to react when it was under attack, after which everyone helped to clear up the mess and repair the damage to ensure that it remained operational.

Many of the airfields that No. 11 Group used during the Battle of Britain date back to the very early days of aviation. The reason for this is quite straightforward: the south of England, with its close proximity to London, witnessed the birth of aviation in Britain. By the time the First World War broke out both the Royal Flying Corps and the Royal Naval Air Service were firmly established in the south. As the air war developed, more airfields were required for the training of pilots and observers, as well as for the preparation of aircraft to make the journey across to France. Furthermore, as the German bombing threat increased, with the introduction of airship and bomber raids on London, more airfields were required for home defence. In particular, the expansion of the Royal Flying Corps from 1916 onwards, followed by the entry of the United States into the war in Europe in 1917, led to plans for more airfields in the south-east of England.

After the First World War many of the airfields were not retained by the newly formed Royal Air Force. Those that did survive were divided into different areas of organization and responsibility, and the airfields of Kent and Sussex fell into No.1 Area. The rapid reduction in the number of airfields led to several variations in area titles and geographic divisions. For example, No. 1 Area became the South-eastern Area, which then merged in 1919 with the South-western Area to form the Southern Area. This in turn merged with the Northern Area in 1920 to become the Inland Area.

Not many airfields covered in this book survived these changes but events in Europe during the 1930s brought several back to life. Following the outbreak of the Second World War, many of the fighter stations were used to support operations in France. Their close proximity to the front line made them ideal for the preparation of fighters before they made the short journey across the Channel. Then, following the fall of France in the spring of 1940, No. 11 Group's airfields were ideally situated to support the evacuation at Dunkirk.

With this background in mind, there is often a pattern to the early history of many of No. 11 Group's airfields, although other sites, not previously used by the military, were often pressed into use as the RAF searched for more airfields during the build-up to the Battle of Britain. When the battle was over most of the airfields were then used by Fighter Command for offensive operations across the Channel. Following entry into the war by the United States an increasing number of airfields in the south-east were used by the Americans, until the Allied landings of 1944 saw a gradual reduction in the number of fighter operations towards the end of the war. Following the end of the Second World War some of the airfields were retained by the RAF; others were not. The history of these sites varies enormously, from those that became international airports to others where there remains little evidence that an airfield existed at all.

This book focuses specifically on events during the summer of 1940, but it also provides a brief history of each airfield, both before and after the Battle of Britain. It is not a detailed history of the battle itself (there is no shortage of books on the subject) but, by way of an introduction to the airfields, it does provide a general overview of No.

11 Group and the battle itself. The airfields are grouped according to sectors of No. 11 Group as they were during the height of the Battle of Britain. This is not always as straightforward as it might sound. For example, Rochford was geographically in the Hornchurch Sector but was used as a satellite airfield for North Weald as well as Hornchurch at various stages during the battle, and Gravesend was geographically in the Hornchurch Sector but was used as a satellite for Biggin Hill. Excluded from the book are Middle Wallop and Filton and their satellites; although these were sector airfields within No. 11 Group on the opening day of the Battle of Britain, they came under the control of the newly formed No. 10 Group just three days after the battle commenced. They are therefore, considered as airfields of No. 10 Group for the purposes of this book.

Needless to say the events of the Battle of Britain meant that the fighter squadrons often moved around as they were either brought into the battle from other parts of the country or moved away from No. 11 Group for a rest. Sometimes, they remained at airfields for just a few days. Every effort has been made to cross-refer dates of moves to as many sources as possible, mainly the original squadron records, but may be a day or so out. Also, the squadron location can be confusing, as the squadron may well have been based at one location but operated out of its satellite or another forward operating airfield on any particular day. It is also difficult cross-referring factual information regarding details of *Luftwaffe* units and losses. Discrepancies are not uncommon and I am sure that most military historians will have been told of their errors on more than one occasion by those that were there at the time! Ultimately, of course, the author has to make a decision but it all contributes to the interest of trying to piece together the day-by-day events.

The book also contains details of some of the places of interest at the various sites. I do not claim to have included them all, but it is perhaps worth mentioning at this point that there is no shortage of information on the internet, where further details about museums and societies can be found. I have summarized the key points of each airfield in the final chapter and have offered my own comments, which I hope you will find useful if you are planning to visit any of the sites. Only time and space prevents more being told but this book will hopefully provide you with enough information to go and visit the sites and experience part of history for yourself. Details of road numbers, opening times and prices of the various museums are correct at the time of writing (summer of 2004), but may have changed.

CHAPTER ONE

NO. 11 GROUP

Before studying the airfields it is important to understand the structure within which No. 11 Group operated during the Battle of Britain. It was part of Fighter Command, which had its headquarters at Bentley Priory just to the north-west of Stanmore in Middlesex. The beautiful grounds there date back to the sixteenth century and the historic building that was used during the Battle of Britain dates back to the 1770s. It had been used as a hotel in the late nineteenth century and as a girls' school in the early 1900s before the Air Ministry took it over in 1926. It became the Headquarters of Fighter Command in 1936.

At the head of Fighter Command was Air Chief Marshal Sir Hugh Dowding. Born in 1882, Hugh Caswall Tremenheere Dowding joined the Army in 1900 and served with the Royal Flying Corps during the First World War. He remained in the post-war RAF and became the Air Officer Commander-in-Chief of Fighter Command when it formed in 1936. At the time of the Battle of Britain he was the most senior serving officer in the RAF at the age of fifty-eight.

During the battle Fighter Command was divided into four groups, each with an Air Vice-Marshal as its Air Officer Commanding (AOC). Each group was split into a number of sectors, which, established geographically, eased the command and control of the bases and fighter squadrons within each group. The responsibility of No. 11 Group was the protection of London and the south-east of England, which meant that it was in the forefront of the battle. To the west of No. 11 Group was the newly formed No. 10 Group, which had the responsibility of protecting the area from mid-Hampshire to the West Country, the industrial part of South Wales and as far north as the southern Midlands.

Air Chief Marshal Sir Hugh Dowding, C-in-C Fighter Command during the Battle of Britain.

No. 12 Group was responsible for the Midlands, the rest of Wales, and the area northwards to a line running across the country from the Lancaster area to just north of Flamborough Head. No. 13 Group covered everything else in the north of England and Scotland. Incidentally, at the end of the Battle of Britain period, the number of groups was increased to six, with No. 9 Group covering the north-west of England and No. 14 Group covering the far north of Scotland. Fighter Command's area of responsibility was essentially overland but extended to 5 miles off the coast, with Coastal Command being responsible for the area beyond.

In command of No. 11 Group was Air Vice-Marshal Keith Park. Born in New Zealand, Keith Rodney Park had served in the Royal Flying Corps during the First World War and as Dowding's Senior Staff Officer in Fighter Command before he was appointed AOC. The group's headquarters was at Uxbridge in Middlesex, about 20 miles to the west of central London, and its responsibility was to protect the south-east of England, which included the area from Harwich south across the Thames estuary to Dover, then westwards along the south coast just beyond Southampton, and northwards to the north-west of London.

Air Vice-Marshal Keith Park, AOC No. 11 Group during the Battle of Britain.

Once France had fallen, one of the major problems facing the group was the exposure of its airfields to air attack. With the *Luftwaffe's* occupation of forward bases in northern France, all of No. 11 Group's airfields were within comfortable range of the German bombers. In June 1940 the Air Staff requested more airfields. For No. 11 Group this meant finding at least one suitable site close to all its recognized airfields, which could either be used as an emergency landing ground or, if necessary, as a base from which operations could be carried out. Initially, the state of the site was not considered overly important. As long as the grass area was long enough and suitably flat for fighters to operate from, the rest could be developed if necessary. Any development, however, would be limited to runway preparation and the provision of basic facilities to ensure that the fighters could be refuelled and rearmed; living and maintenance had to be managed as best as possible.

At the beginning of July 1940 there were eight sector airfields in No. 11 Group, which formed a formidable line of defence from the north-east of London to the south-west of England. The airfields were: North Weald (Essex), Hornchurch (east of central London), Biggin Hill (Kent), Kenley (Surrey), Tangmere (West Sussex), Middle Wallop (Hampshire), Northolt (west of central London) and Filton (Bristol). Within days of the battle opening the number of sectors was reduced to seven. Middle Wallop and Filton (Sectors W and Y respectively) were both transferred to the newly formed No. 10 Group, and Debden (Sector F to the north-east of London) was transferred to No. 11 Group from No. 12 Group.

Air Chief Marshal Sir Hugh Dowding			
10 Group	**11 Group**	**12 Group**	**13 Group**
AVM Sir Quintin Brand	AVM K.R. Park	AVM T.L Leigh-Mallory	AVM R.E.Saul
Middle Wallop	Tangmere	Coltishall	Catterick
Filton	Kenley	Duxford	Usworth
	Biggin Hill	Wittering	Acklington
	Hornchurch	Digby	Turnhouse
	North Weald	Kirton-in-Lindsey	Dyce
	Debden	Church Fenton	Wick
	Northolt		

Fighter Command Structure and Sector Airfields, August 1940.

No.11 Group & Sector Airfields – August 1940

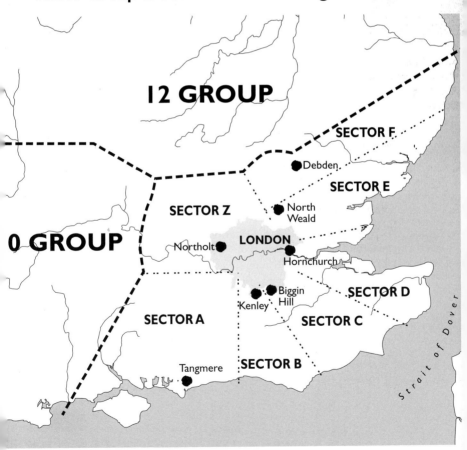

The sector airfields of No. 11 Group that did not have them rapidly gained satellite airfields, advanced landing grounds or relief landing grounds. Although these often began as simply large grass areas, many were soon transformed into airfields with facilities for the permanent accommodation of either small detachments of aircraft and personnel or complete squadrons.

Every effort was made to confuse the Germans, including camouflaging airfields and constructing decoys complete with wooden aircraft and dummy flare paths. Examples of these during the Battle of Britain were at Barnet, to the north of London, where a dummy airfield was created on the local golf course, and at Lullingstone to the north-east of Biggin Hill. Camouflage, in particular, was given a high priority and various techniques were used to break up the shape of aircraft hangars, key buildings and the airfield itself. Those that had hard runways and aircraft aprons were treated so that the hard surfaces were 'textured' to prevent them from standing out when seen from a bomber at medium altitude. There were also examples of local innovation. For example, an airfield surrounded by housing was often camouflaged so that hangars and technical buildings looked like houses. The idea was to make the airfield blend in with the surroundings as much as possible. It was, of course, fully accepted that to try and hide an airfield and prevent an attack by day in good weather conditions was difficult, but the idea was simply to cause doubt in the minds of the bomber crew about the location, size and aspect of the target. This could all result in a vital delay in a bomber releasing its bomb load and therefore prevent it from hitting its target. Although the camouflage of airfields continued until about 1943, the need for decoy airfields was rather more short-term, as by the end of the Battle of Britain the *Luftwaffe* had taken to bombing at night rather than by day.

The Aircraft

As No. 11 Group was in the forefront of Britain's defence, it had more squadrons then any other group. When the Battle of Britain opened, it had approximately 350 aircraft and twenty-two squadrons: thirteen equipped with Hurricanes, five with Spitfires, three with Blenheims and one with Defiants.

The Hawker Hurricane was designed by Sydney Camm and first flew in November 1935. The first aircraft entered service at the end of 1937 and by early 1940 more than 600 were in service with the RAF. The Hurricane I was powered by a Rolls-Royce Merlin engine and armed with eight 0.303 in Browning machine guns, four in each wing.

The Hurricane was flown in greater numbers during the battle than any other RAF fighter.

It had a maximum speed of 335 mph at 18,000 ft and an operating ceiling of 35,000 ft. It took about six and a half minutes to reach operating height of 15,000 ft. Tactically, because of the Hurricane's inferior performance to the Bf 109, the best results were achieved against the *Luftwaffe* bombers, leaving the Spitfires to engage the escorting fighters.

The Spitfire was designed by Reginald Mitchell and first flew in March 1936. It entered service with the RAF during 1938, and there were many similarities with the Hurricane; the engine and armament, for example, were the same. However, the aerodynamic design and lower wing loading of the Spitfire gave it better performance and a greater turning advantage. More importantly, it meant that the Spitfire was more manoeuvrable than the Bf109 at all heights. It had a top speed of over 350 mph at 19,000 ft and an operating ceiling of 34,000 ft. It could reach an operating height of 20,000 ft in about nine minutes. Production figures for the Spitfire during 1940 were not as high as for the Hurricane (about eighty per month compared to a peak of nearly 250 per month for the Hurricane), which meant that there were fewer Spitfire squadrons during the Battle of Britain – although the Spitfire accounted for more than half of Fighter Command's successes.

The Bristol Blenheim IF was used as a night fighter, even though it had been designed as a high-speed light bomber. It first flew in 1936 and was powered by two Bristol Mercury engines, which gave it a speed of up to 275 mph at 15,000 ft and an operational ceiling of

17

25,000 ft. It was fitted with a semi-retractable, hydraulically operated dorsal turret with a single Vickers K gun. Because it had suffered losses during daylight operations over France, it was only used at night during the Battle of Britain, as it was considered to be no match for the Bf109. In the night fighter role it was converted from the standard Mk I aircraft to the Mk IF by the addition of four 0.303 in Browning machine guns mounted in a ventral pack under the centre fuselage. The development of airborne radar led to its installation in the Blenheim IF and there was the occasional success.

The fourth fighter used during the battle was the Boulton Paul Defiant I, which first flew in 1937. Initially its performance was considered to be very good in terms of speed and flying characteristics. It was powered by a Merlin engine, as fitted to the Spitfire and Hurricane, and could achieve a speed of just over 300 mph at 17,000 ft, with an operating ceiling of 30,000 ft. It entered operational service with the RAF early in 1940 and it was involved in the air war over France. Two squadrons were equipped with the Defiant during the Battle of Britain but its performance proved to be one of the biggest disappointments to Fighter Command; it suffered disastrous losses when up against the Bf109. Its concept of operating as a two crew aircraft (pilot and air gunner) proved problematic, it had no forward firing armament but instead had a hydraulically operated rear-mounted turret with four 0.303 inch Browning machine guns. It was up to the pilot to position the aircraft and the gunner to bring its armament to bear. Following disastrous losses it was soon withdrawn from daylight operations, but it did later operate at night.

Defiants of No. 264 Sqn. The combination of the lack of forward firing armament and poor performance led to disastrous losses for Defiant crews when up against the Bf109.

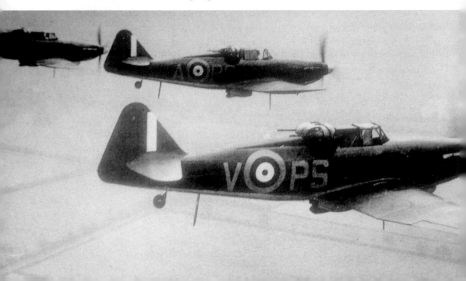

Armourers re-arming a Hurricane.

Britain's Defence System

The technical development of radar had provided Britain with the capability of early warning of attack, which compensated for the RAF's numerical disadvantage. This meant that the RAF could avoid having fighters continuously in the air over southern England to protect its Channel ports, airfields, industrial installations, and the south's heavily populated towns and cities. This would not only have proved costly in vital resources such as fuel but increasing fatigue would gradually have drained the pilots over a period of time. However, pilots had to be kept at readiness, which made it essential for No. 11 Group to keep all its airfields open.

By July 1940 a chain of detection stations had been established between the north-east and south-west of Britain, known as Chain Home. The transmitter aerials were on steel towers about 350 ft high and the receivers were on wooden towers about 240 ft high. Detection was possible out to a range of about 100 miles, depending on the height of the aircraft. However, detection of low flying aircraft was not possible and so Chain Home Low was developed with a range of up to 50 miles, although the height of aircraft could not be accurately determined. The aerials detected formations of aircraft as they formed up across the Channel over northern France. The operator was

19

presented with a V-shaped 'blip' on a cathode ray tube display in a building known as the Receiver Block. From there information was passed to the Filter Room at Bentley Priory and then to No. 11 Group at Uxbridge. It was from there that the duty controller would alert the appropriate sector airfield, which then scrambled and directed the various squadrons. The system and process was designed so that the time taken from receipt of a radar 'blip' to alerting the squadron best placed to deal with the threat was less than six minutes. It is also worth mentioning at this point that by the beginning of the Battle of Britain all of Fighter Command's fighters had been fitted with Identification Friend-or-Foe (IFF) to help avoid confusion between 'friendlies' and 'hostiles'.

There were sixteen radar sites within No. 11 Group's area of responsibility, eight of which were high level sites (Chain Home or CH) and eight low-level (Chain Home Low or CHL). From Suffolk, working clockwise they were: Dunwich (CHL), High Street (CH), Bawdsey (CH), Bromley (CH), Walton (CHL), Canewdon (CH),

Below: There were a number of Chain Home sites within No. 11 Group's area of responsibility, including this one at Poling in Sussex.

Right: Remaining transmitter aerials at the Dover radar site, which is passed on the A2 just to the north-east of the town.

Dunkirk (CH), Foreness (CHL), Dover (CHL), Rye (CH), Fairlight (CHL), Pevensey (CH), Beachy Head (CHL), Truleigh (CHL), Poling (CHL) and Ventnor on the Isle of Wight (CH).

In addition to the radar sites, the Observer Corps also watched the skies over southern England. They used binoculars to spot the small specks in the sky, which grew increasingly larger as formations of enemy aircraft approached. They communicated by telephone with the Observer Corps centres and provided warning of attack, giving numbers, heights and types of enemy aircraft. Used with the information provided by the early-warning radar sites, and any information from patrolling fighters, this was a vital input to help develop the air picture. The accuracy of the Observer Corps input to the overall air picture depended mostly on visual information and was obviously restricted during cloudy conditions or at night. But all this information had to be put together to make sure that the fighters were in the right place at the right time.

The heart of Britain's defence system was Fighter Command's filter room at Bentley Priory. Information from the various sources was presented on a large plotting table showing an outline map with an arrangement of coloured discs to represent enemy formations. Red, yellow or blue were used to represent periods of time, each of five minutes, so that controllers could tell the history of the tracks, which would never be more than fifteen minutes old. Woman's Auxiliary Air Force personnel (WAAFs) moved the counters around the plotting table using magnetic rakes. Sitting above the plotting table and watching over events was the duty controller and other officers with telephones connecting the filter room with Group headquarters.

Information would pass from Bentley Priory to Uxbridge, which in turn passed the relevant information to the appropriate sector airfields (each with its own operations room), which then alerted the squadrons. Known affectionately as 'the hole', the air-conditioned operations room at Uxbridge had been constructed two storeys underground. It was relatively compact and measured 60 ft across. The duty controller sat on a raised dais next to a bank of telephones, which linked the sector airfields. On the opposite wall was a status panel, which had light bulbs to show the status of every squadron within the group. Again, a colour system was used to show the duty controller the history of the information, which again was never more than fifteen minutes old. The WAAF plotters listened through headphones and marked the state of the air battle on a large map below, using long croupier rods to move the various coloured discs around the map. A four-watch system

The Operations Room at Bentley Priory.

was used for those working in the bunker, with individuals on an eight-hour shift during the 24-hour period, with one shift off at any one time.

Throughout the period of the battle, squadrons were rotated depending on their strength at any one time and dispersed assets when the airfields became priority targets. Those squadrons in the forefront of the action often moved several times. Nevertheless, the RAF maintained the advantage of operating close to home. Its fighters could land back at base, or elsewhere if necessary, to refuel and rearm, and then be back in the air in a relatively short space of time. Readiness states of the squadrons varied; the highest was 'stand by', with the pilot in the cockpit facing into the wind ready to start his engine immediately and take off. The obvious disadvantage for the pilot was that he was often sitting in a very warm cockpit and was not able to stretch out or relax, which meant that this state of readiness could only be maintained for short periods at a time. The next state was 'at readiness', with the pilots at the squadron dispersal, ready to be airborne within five minutes. The more relaxed state was 'available thirty minutes' with the pilots at the Mess, ready to be airborne within thirty minutes.

Britain's defence system also included searchlights and anti-aircraft guns to defend the cities, plus many lighter guns to protect the airfields. Anti-aircraft Command was under the command of Lieutenant-General Sir Frederick Pile, and had its headquarters at Stanmore. Responsibility for the protection of London belonged to the 1st Anti-aircraft Division, with more than 120 heavy guns. The rest of the south-east was the responsibility of the 6th Anti-aircraft Division, with nearly 200 heavy guns, mainly old 3 in guns plus the newer 3.7 in and 4.5 in ones. In addition there were a few hundred more light guns (mainly two-pounders and Bofors 40 mm) and several hundred light machine-guns protecting the airfields and other key targets.

No. 30 (Balloon Barrage) Group was also responsible for the protection of London and the south-east of England with more than 500 balloons, which were able to reach heights of up to 5,000 ft. They were not there in the hope that an attacking aircraft would fly into one, or its cables, but more to keep them at height so that bombing accuracy was more difficult. During the period of the Battle of Britain, bombing techniques from medium level were basic. Whilst the *Luftwaffe* crews could attempt to put bombs within an airfield boundary, there was no guarantee of hitting any specific targets such as runways, hangars or technical buildings. Even leaving craters across the airfield would not necessarily prevent fighter operations. However, attacks from low level caused most damage, and it was necessary for No. 11 Group's airfields to have good defences.

Whilst the number and type of defences varied from airfield to

The airfield defences were vital. This gun emplacement was at Croydon.

airfield, those at Kenley provide a good example. Its main airfield defences consisted of two 3 in anti-aircraft guns manned by the 148th Light Anti-aircraft Battery, four smaller 40 mm Bofors guns manned by the 31st Light Anti-aircraft Battery and several Lewis machine guns. There was also a parachute and cable installation, known as PAC, which fired salvos of rockets at any raiders at low level. The rockets were designed to reach a height of about 500–700 ft. The parachutes would slow down the rate of descent of the steel cables and the hope was that low-flying aircraft would fly into them. PAC did have some success and it is credited with bringing down a Do17 in a low-level attack against Kenley during the early afternoon of 18 August. In addition to the one brought down, a second was hit and crashed near Biggin Hill. The Dorniers then came under attack by Hurricanes and two ditched in the Channel on the way home, two force-landed in France and three more returned to base damaged. Although these successes cannot be credited to the Kenley defences, any damage to a German bomber, no matter how slight, would have improved the chances of the RAF fighters: one of the crew being hit, so that the aircraft was not able to fully defend itself; the aircraft being hit and damage caused to one of its flying control surfaces, in which case the aircraft was unable to manoeuvre defensively; one of the engines being hit, in which case the aircraft would lose power and not be able to climb or maintain speed; the aircraft losing fuel, which would give the bomber crew the difficult choice of escaping at high speed and not being able to make it home or reducing speed to ensure the aircraft could make it back to base but being vulnerable to the RAF's fighters. Whatever the reason, any success by the airfield's defences helped the overall aim of preventing the bombers from returning another day.

In addition to the airfield defences were the local defences. All along the coastline of south-east England there were the Home Defences, although only one in three individuals had a rifle. The Army was not in a much better position, with so much equipment having been lost during evacuation from Dunkirk. There was just one machine gun for every mile along the coast but every possible way of obstructing an enemy invasion and subsequent advance was used.

CHAPTER TWO

THE BATTLE OF BRITAIN

Historians have often debated the official dates of the Battle of Britain. According to the Air Ministry (and later the Ministry of Defence) the battle opened on 10 July and closed on 31 October 1940. Others have suggested that the opening of the battle was either 8 or 11 August and the close either 15 September or 5 October. These dates are certainly more representative of the period of sustained air fighting but for the purposes of this work the Ministry's official dates of 10 July to 31 October are used.

The French surrender on 22 June 1940 meant that Britain stood alone. For Dowding the situation was desperate. The loss of so many fighters and, more importantly, many of his most experienced pilots, meant that Fighter Command needed time to recover. Fortunately, the German advance stopped at the Channel, as Hitler believed that there might be a peaceful solution to the war in the west. These vital few weeks gave Britain the chance to prepare and Fighter Command the chance to train new pilots. Soon Dowding had the over fifty squadrons that he felt were essential if Britain was to stand any chance of survival.

When it became obvious that there was to be no peaceful solution, Hitler ordered preparations to be put in place for an invasion of England. First, however, it was necessary for the *Luftwaffe* to gain air superiority over the Channel to minimize losses.

The *Luftwaffe*

Based in northern France and the Low Countries, the *Luftwaffe* was commanded by *Reichsmarschall* Hermann Goering. Full of confidence following Germany's victories in Europe, the *Luftwaffe* was made up of air fleets (*Luftflotten*). Based in the north-east of France, Belgium, Holland and north-west Germany were the units of *Luftflotte* 2 commanded by *Generalfeldmarschall* Albert Kesselring. The units of *Luftflotte* 3 were based in northern and western France under the command of *Generalfeldmarschall* Hugo Sperrle. Each *Luftflotte* consisted of one or more *Fliegerkorps*. Under *Luftflotte* 2 was

Reichsmarschall **Hermann Goering, commander of the** *Luftwaffe*.

Fliegerkorps I (north-east France), *Fliegerkorps* II (Belgium) and *Fliegerkorps* IX (Holland and north-west Germany). *Luftflotte* 3 consisted of *Fliegerkorps* IV (Brittany area), *Fliegerkorps* V (Seine area) and *Fliegerkorps* VIII (Cherbourg area). In addition were the units of *Luftflotte* 5, which consisted of *Fliegerkorps* X based in Norway and Denmark under the command of *Generaloberst* Hans-Jurgen Stumpf. The operational units were the *Geshwaders* and each *Fliegerkorps* had its own bomber (*Kampfgeschwader* – KG), dive-bomber (*Stukageschwader* – StG), fighter (*Jagdgeschwader* – JG or *Zerstörergeschwader* – ZG) and long-range reconnaissance (*Aufklärungsgruppe* – Aukfl) units.

The *Luftwaffe*'s principal fighter, and the RAF's toughest adversary, was the Messerschmitt Bf109E, which operated with the various *Jagdgeschwaders* of *Luftflotten* 2 and 3. It was powered by a Daimler-Benz engine with fuel injection, which gave it an advantage in either the zero or negative 'G' environment. This meant that it could out-dive its opponents, although both the Spitfire and the Hurricane had a better turning performance. The Bf109E was armed with two 20 mm cannons (one in each wing) and two fuselage-mounted 7.9 mm machine guns (which fired through the propeller). It had a maximum speed of just over 350 mph at 18,000 ft and its operating ceiling was 35,000 ft. During the Battle of Britain the *Luftwaffe* had 700–800 Bf109s available at any one time. Whilst over southern England it could operate for about twenty minutes, less if it was operating as far as London. It was mainly used to counter the Spitfires and Hurricanes,

The Messerschmitt Bf109E was the *Luftwaffe*'s principal fighter during the Battle of Britain and was responsible for most of Fighter Command's losses.

which left the less capable Bf110 to escort the bombers. However, through necessity, *Luftwaffe* tactics later changed, as more responsibility was placed on the Bf109 pilots to help protect the bombers. This meant that the Bf109E pilots were unable to exploit their speed advantage fully, particularly over the Hurricane, and Bf109 losses gradually increased, although they were responsible for most of Fighter Command's losses during the battle.

The *Luftwaffe's* other fighter during the Battle of Britain was the Messerschmitt Bf110C, which had a crew of two (pilot and air gunner) and was designed as a twin-engined high-performance fighter. Powered by two Daimler-Benz engines it could reach a maximum speed of just under 350 mph at 23,000 ft and had an operating ceiling of 33,000 ft. It was armed with two 20 mm cannons, four forward-firing 7.9 mm machine-guns and an aft-mounted machine-gun in the rear cockpit. Tactically it had been designed to destroy the enemy's fighter defences (evident by its name *Zerstörer* or 'Destroyer') but it was always expected to operate in areas where the *Luftwaffe* had air superiority. At the beginning of the Battle of Britain the *Luftwaffe* had about 270 BF110Cs, of which some 200 were available at any one time. Its performance during the battle was one of the *Luftwaffe's* biggest disappointments, as it lacked speed and manoeuvrability, which meant that it suffered heavy losses and it was increasingly used as a fighter-bomber and for reconnaissance duties.

The *Luftwaffe* had a number of bombers available to it during the battle. When the battle opened the Heinkel He111 represented more than half of its operational strength of just over 1,000 twin-engined bombers. The two main variants were the He111P (powered by Daimler-Benz engines) and the He111H (powered by Jumo engines). It had a crew of either four or five (pilot, navigator/bombardier, radio operator and air gunner(s)), and could carry eight bombs, each 250 kg (550 lb) and stored internally and stowed vertically, which limited the He111's effectiveness as a bomber. Its defensive armament was up to seven 7.9 mm machine-guns (depending on the variant), which were mounted at various points around the fuselage. The He111H could achieve a speed of up to 240 mph at 15,000 ft and it had an operational ceiling of 26,000 ft. A high number of losses led to the He111 being

When the battle opened the He111 represented more than half of the *Luftwaffe's* operational strength of twin-engine bombers.

The Do17Z was well liked by its crews and quickly gained the reputation of being the *Luftwaffe*'s most reliable bomber during the Battle of Britain.

withdrawn from daylight operations and it became increasingly used at night towards the end of the battle.

The Dornier Do17Z was well liked by its crews and it quickly gained the reputation of being the *Luftwaffe*'s most reliable bomber during the Battle of Britain. Its design meant that its bomb load was limited to a total of 1,000 kg (2,200 lb). It had a crew of four, defensive armament of between four and eight 7.9 mm machine-guns (depending on local modifications at unit level) and uprated BMW Bramo engines. Its performance was limited and it could generally only achieve a speed of just over 250 mph at its operating ceiling of 21,000 ft. However, in a shallow dive attack it could achieve speeds up to 370 mph.

During the Battle of Britain, there were about 500 Do17Zs operating with nine KGs. Despite the increase in its defensive armament the design of the aircraft meant that it remained vulnerable to attack from behind and below. Nevertheless, it was more manoeuvrable than other German bombers, which meant that it could often make its attack, and escape, at low level. However, losses were high and the number involved was gradually reduced towards the end of the battle.

The newest of the *Luftwaffe*'s bombers to participate in the Battle of Britain was the Junkers Ju88A. It was designed as a high-speed

Spitfires of No. 610 Sqn based at Biggin Hill during July 1940. The Spitfire captured the hearts of the British nation and became a legend following the Battle of Britain.

bomber and had a crew of four. It was powered by two Jumo engines, which gave it a better performance than the other German bombers, and was capable of 290 mph at 15,000 ft and an operating ceiling of 23,000 ft. It could carry an internal bomb load of up to twenty-eight 50 kg (110 lb) bombs. Two external hard points beneath each wing meant that the aircraft was also capable of carrying two 500 kg bombs externally, although only two 100 kg bombs could be carried externally when the aircraft was carrying a maximum internal bomb load. By mid-August 1940 three KGs were equipped with the Ju88A but the aircraft lacked good defensive armament, which meant that it suffered considerable losses. It was only fitted with three 7.9 mm machine-guns and, like the Do17Z, its design meant that it was vulnerable to attack from the rear and from below. Nevertheless, its speed often gave it the chance to escape.

Another great disappointment

The Ju87B 'Stuka' was used extensively during the main attacks on radar sites in August 1940 but high losses led to it soon being withdrawn from the battle.

for the *Luftwaffe* during the Battle of Britain was the performance of the Junkers Ju87 Stuka (from *Sturzkampflugzeug*, a name given to all dive-bombers). It was powered by a Jumo engine, was capable of speeds of up to 250 mph at 15,000 ft, and its operating ceiling was 23,000 ft. With a crew of two (pilot and air gunner), the Ju87B could carry a single 500 kg bomb (1,100 lb) under the fuselage and four 50 kg (110 lb) bombs under the wings. It was armed with two forward firing 7.9 mm machine-guns (one in each wing) and a single aft-mounted 7.9 mm machine-gun for the gunner. When the battle opened the *Luftwaffe's Stukagruppen* (StGs) had just over 300 Stukas, of which about 250 were available at any one time. Although used during the early attacks on shipping convoys in the Channel, the Ju87B Stuka was essentially used operationally for just eleven days during August, when it was used extensively during the main attacks on radar sites and airfields along the south coast. However, it suffered from a lack of speed and manoeuvrability, and high losses led to it soon being withdrawn from the battle.

The Battle

The Battle of Britain officially opened on Wednesday, 10 July 1940. This date does not mark any specific event other than the air fighting over the British convoy 'Bread' during the early afternoon but has since denoted the opening of the greatest air battle in history. The *Luftwaffe's* main priority during the first few weeks was to destroy shipping in the Channel, and the attacks against the convoys continued throughout July. By the beginning of August the *Luftwaffe* extended its bombing operations by night to towns and cities. On 8 August the convoy CW9, codenamed 'Peewit', was attacked several times during the day off the Isle of Wight, and this resulted in the heaviest air fighting to date; thirty-one *Luftwaffe* aircraft were destroyed for the loss of twenty RAF fighters.

The battle then entered a new phase as the German high command changed its priorities to attacking the radar stations and the airfields of Fighter Command. On 13 August the *Luftwaffe* launched its new offensive, *Adlertag* 'Eagle Day' but it got off to a disastrous start amidst confusion during the early morning. The weather forecast had predicted low cloud and drizzle, and Goering gave the order to postpone *Adlertag* until later in the day. However, the order did not reach all the units and shortly after 5.00 a.m. the first aircraft took off to attack targets in south-east England. Owing to the weather the attacks were carried out at low level with some success, although several bombers were shot down. Goering was furious at the confusion and ordered *Adlertag* to commence properly during the afternoon. The first large raid of more than 300 aircraft crossed the Channel at 3.30 p.m. to attack targets in south-east England. As the day ended, the night offensive continued with a number of raids against targets all over the country.

During the following few days the *Luftwaffe* carried out its attacks on a wide front, the main targets being the radar stations and the airfields of Fighter Command. Heavy attacks on 24 August marked the start of a new and more determined series of raids against these airfields, which stretched the pilots and ground crews of No. 11 Group to the limits. That night, the first bombs fell on London.

The Battle of Britain reached its height during the last two weeks of August and early September. The total strength of both sides varied from day to day but, typically, the *Luftwaffe* had approximately 3,500 front-line aircraft, of which more than 2,500 were available at any one time. This can be broken down simply to about 1,000 bombers, 1,000 fighters, 250 dive-bombers and 250 reconnaissance aircraft of various types. The number of daily sorties flown averaged well over 1,000, with peaks on 13 August (approximately 1,500), 15 August (2,100), 16 August (1,700) and 31 August (1,500). Fighter Command had about 700 fighters and 1,400 pilots available and on one occasion, on 30

The ground crew worked tirelessly to keep the airfields operational during the height of the *Luftwaffe*'s attacks in August.

August, managed 1,000 sorties in a day; it was also not far short of 1,000 sorties on 15 August and 31 August.

Fighter Command's gallant young fighter pilots were shooting down large numbers of German aircraft, but RAF losses were also high. Furthermore, there had been significant damage to many of No. 11 Group's airfields. The aircraft production lines were working hard to maintain the balance between the number of fighters shot down and new aircraft to replace them. However, the loss of pilots was beginning to tell. Although many escaped with their lives, a large number were either badly burned or wounded and were unable to make an immediate return to the front line. More young men replaced them, but most had very few flying hours to prepare for battle. Until early September Dowding had been able to rotate his squadrons, sending the pilots north for a well-earned rest, but as the losses mounted this became less of an option.

On 7 September a new phase of the battle began, when the *Luftwaffe* unexpectedly turned to bombing London. Despite the losses to the RAF and civilians alike, this change of tactics gave the airfields of Fighter Command the rest so desperately needed. The German invasion of England had been set for 20 September and time was getting short. A major effort was made by the *Luftwaffe* on 15 September, the day that was later to become celebrated as 'Battle of Britain' day.

It so happened that Winston Churchill visited the Operations Room at Uxbridge that morning. The day started quietly as the local population across southern England made their way to church – typical of any other Sunday morning. However, at Uxbridge the battle was beginning to unfold. Soon after 11.00 a.m. the first squadrons were airborne and by 11.25 a.m. all of No. 11 Group's squadrons were in the air. One by one the red bulbs next to each squadron on the

King George VI (left), accompanied by Air Chief Marshal Sir Hugh Dowding, in the rear gardens of Bentley Priory during his visit on 6 September 1940.

status panel illuminated as they intercepted the enemy. Although all the squadrons were airborne, some could only muster a handful of aircraft; in the most extreme case, one squadron had just two Hurricanes airborne.

An hour later it was over – but there was more to come. Soon after 1.00 p.m. the picture began to build once more as the first of the German raiders formed up over northern France. By 2.00 p.m. the fighters were airborne once more and within minutes the air battle had recommenced. No. 11 Group had put every available fighter into the air and the light bulbs on the status panel were, once again, a sea of red. It was at this point that Churchill asked Air Vice-Marshal Keith Park, 'What reserves are there?'; Park's famous reply was 'There are none.' By 3.50 p.m. it was all over. The future of Britain had hung in the balance and in the hands of the young men who had so bravely fought the greatest of air battles. Winston Churchill left soon after. It was several hours before No. 11 Group and Fighter Command could make any real sense of the outcome of the day's air battle. No one at that time could know the significance of the day's events and what effect it would have on the Battle of Britain and, indeed, the rest of the war.

The underground bunker and operations room can still be seen at RAF Uxbridge today. It has been restored to the way it was at 11.30 a.m. on Sunday 15 September. Visits are by prior arrangement and anyone interested should contact the Curator, Chris Wren, on 01895 815400 or by fax on 01895 815666. Visitors should not arrive at the main entrance to RAF Uxbridge without prior permission.

Although 15 September 1940 was not the most successful day for Fighter Command in terms of the number of enemy aircraft shot down,

This Bf109 failed to make it back across the Channel.

the RAF's famous victory in the air on that day did mark the beginning
of the end of the Battle of Britain. The mood on the two sides of the
Channel was quite different; a sense of victory for the RAF but one of
dismay for the Germans. Within forty-eight hours Hitler had postponed
his planned invasion of England – indefinitely.

The final phase of the battle began on 1 October with another
change in *Luftwaffe* tactics. Although the night raids against London
and the other large towns and cities continued, the mass daylight raids
against London ceased. The last phase consisted of several small
daylight incursions against southern England, many of which were
carried out by modified Bf109s capable of carrying either long-range
fuel tanks or a single 250 kg (55 lb) bomb. These generally proved to
be nothing more than nuisance raids; their main aim was to keep the
defences split over a large area in preperation of the main German
offensive against England the following spring.

The Battle of Britain officially ended on Thursday, 31 October, but
the incursions across southern England and the night raids on London
continued for several months. Official German records for August and
September 1940 show total *Luftwaffe* losses as 953; 348 bombers, 47
dive-bombers and 558 fighters. The highest *Luftwaffe* losses occurred
on 15 August (55 aircraft destroyed) and 15 September (56 aircraft
destroyed). RAF losses for the same period were also high; 715
fighters destroyed, with peaks on 15 August (34) and 31 August (39).

Nearly 500 of Fighter Command's pilots had been killed, were missing or taken prisoner during the course of the battle and another 400 had been wounded or injured.

To sum up the reason why the *Luftwaffe* was not successful in defeating the RAF during the summer of 1940, it is probably because it was a very capable tactical air force but not capable of succeeding in a strategic campaign. It did, however, come close. The cost to Fighter Command had been high but Britain's safety had been assured, at least for the time being, which meant that valuable support could be given elsewhere.

The underground Operations Room at Uxbridge has been restored to how it was at 11.30 a.m. on 15 September 1940.

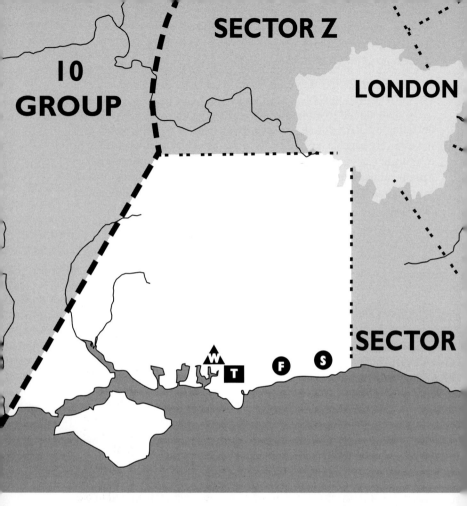

SECTOR Z

10
GROUP

LONDON

SECTOR

SECTOR A – AUGUST 1940

KEY:-

T = Tangmere, Sector Airfield

W = Westhampnett, Satellite Airfield

F = Ford, Royal Navy (FAA) Airfield

S = Shoreham, Advanced Operating Airfield

CHAPTER THREE

TANGMERE SECTOR
SECTOR A

The most western area for which No. 11 Group was responsible for was the Tangmere Sector, or Sector A, which marked the boundary between it and No. 10 Group. It covered the largest overland area in No. 11 Group's area of responsibility and was bounded to the west by an imaginary line from Reading south-west to Bournemouth, including the Isle of Wight. From Reading the sector boundary ran east to the edge of London and then south to Brighton. There were Observer Corps centres near Winchester and Horsham and large anti-aircraft batteries at Southampton, Portsmouth, Bramley near Basingstoke, and Brooklands, as well as balloon barrages at Southampton and Thorney Island. The areas within the sector that were of greatest interest to the *Luftwaffe* were the ports of Southampton and Portsmouth, the radar sites at Poling and Ventnor on the Isle of Wight, several factories and, of course, the airfields.

No. 11 Group's two airfields within the Tangmere Sector were both in West Sussex, just to the north-east of Chichester. One was the RAF station at Tangmere itself and the other was its satellite at nearby Westhampnett. During the Battle of Britain No. 11 Group also used Shoreham, just to the west of Brighton, as an advanced operating airfield and the naval airfield at Ford in West Sussex. Although Ford was a Royal Navy base for most of the battle, it was transferred to No. 11 Group towards the end. For completeness, therefore, brief details of both Shoreham and Ford are included in this chapter. However, neither of the airfields at Merston, which was being developed as a satellite for Tangmere, and Pulborough, which was being developed as an emergency landing ground for Tangmere, were completed in time for the Battle of Britain and these are, therefore, both excluded.

Although not part of No. 11 Group there are four other airfields within the sector (all in Hampshire) that are of interest to the Battle of Britain. Eastleigh was where the prototype Spitfire made its first flight in March 1936, and it was used by Spitfires of No. 266 Squadron for two days during August 1940; it was even attacked by the *Luftwaffe* on 24 August. Thorney Island belonged to Coastal Command and was used by Blenheims of Nos 235 and 236 Squadrons, which provided convoy patrols over the Channel during the early weeks of the battle. Although these squadrons were both Coastal Command units, they are both officially recognized as having taken part in the Battle of Britain. German intelligence certainly recognized the importance of Thorney Island and included it in its attacks on Fighter Command's airfields. There were minor attacks on 13 and 16 August and a major one on 18 August, which caused considerable damage.

The other two airfields of interest were Gosport, a Coastal Command airfield just to the west of Portsmouth, and the Royal Navy airfield at Lee-on-Solent. Although Gosport was not used for air operations during the Battle of Britain the airfield did suffer attacks on 12, 16 and 18 August, which caused considerable damage, and Lee-on-Solent also suffered an attack on 16 August.

Tangmere

Three miles north-east of Chichester, Tangmere was one of Fighter Command's most famous airfields during the Battle of Britain. Its history goes back to the later years of the First World War when, quite by accident, a civilian pilot flying from Shoreham had to make a forced landing at what was then Bayleys Farm. The original airfield was constructed on 200 acres of land. Work to prepare the site began in late 1917 and various British units used the airfield during the summer of 1918 before it was handed to the Americans as the war was coming to a close. With the war over, the Americans departed and Tangmere became a holding station for units returning from France.

In 1920 the airfield closed but the Air Ministry retained the land. The large hangars and sheds were suitable as storage units and Tangmere reopened in 1925 as a Coastal Area unit. The airfield was made active once more and No. 43 Squadron moved in with Gamecocks the following year, followed soon after by Siskins of No. 1 Squadron. Improvements to the buildings and facilities were completed in the early 1930s, by which time both squadrons had re-equipped with the Fury. The station remained one of the most popular establishments during the mid-1930s. Both squadrons were long-term residents there and the rivalry between them seemed to make Tangmere popular amongst its personnel.

The RAF's expansion scheme during 1936–7 brought rapid changes to Tangmere as new squadrons appeared. By mid-1939 there had been considerable changes. The airfield had been extended to the east to provide greater runway length, and a hardened perimeter track had been constructed. There had also been considerable improvement to the buildings and support facilities, as well as air raid shelters. New fighters had also arrived during the later months of 1938, with both No. 1 and No. 43 Squadrons re-equipping with the RAF's newest fighter, the Hurricane.

When the Second World War was declared Hurricanes and Gladiators of No. 605 Squadron arrived to replace No. 1 Squadron, which was destined for France as part of the Advanced Air Striking Force. The phoney war lasted for several months and there were several 'comings and goings' between various squadrons and units. Life remained reasonably quiet at Tangmere until the Germans launched their attack against France and the Low Countries in May 1940. At that time, the airfield was home to Nos 501 and 601 Squadrons, and both these units were sent across the Channel to France.

When the Battle of Britain opened Tangmere was the sector airfield for Sector A and was home to four Hurricane squadrons and six Blenheims of the Fighter Interception Unit (FIU). The Hurricane squadrons were Nos 145 and 43, which had both arrived in May, and Nos 601 and 1, which had arrived in June. During the first few weeks of the battle, all four were involved in air activities over the Channel. The first losses from Tangmere were two Hurricanes, one from No. 145 Squadron and one from No. 601 Squadron, which were both shot down over the Channel during the early evening of 11 July; both pilots survived.

During the late afternoon of 19 July No. 43 Squadron was involved in heavy fighting with Bf109s of JG27 off Selsey Bill, and two Hurricanes were shot down. One of the pilots, Sergeant James Buck, became the first Tangmere pilot to be killed during the battle. Although he managed to bale out, he had been wounded during the attack and drowned.

One of the squadron's pilots involved in the action of 19 July was Flight Lieutenant Frank Carey, who destroyed a Bf109 off Selsey Bill and damaged two others. Born in London, he joined the RAF in 1927. He first served with No. 43 Squadron at Tangmere as a metal rigger in 1930, and rejoined the squadron in 1936 as a sergeant pilot. After a short period with No. 3 Squadron in France, he returned to No. 43 Squadron in June 1940 as a flight commander. By then, he had been awarded the DFM and the DFC and bar for the destruction of thirteen enemy aircraft. Whilst serving with No. 43 Squadron during the Battle of Britain, he brought his total to nineteen, and by the end of the war he had destroyed twenty-five enemy aircraft, for which he was awarded a second bar to his DFC. He did all this whilst flying Hurricanes, making him the RAF's second highest Hurricane ace of the war.

The following day, on 20 July, No. 43 Squadron lost another pilot when Flying Officer Joseph Haworth was shot down south of the Needles. Although he was seen to bale out, his body was never found and he is remembered on the Runnymede Memorial. The squadron suffered its third loss in three days when Pilot Officer Ricardo de Mancha collided with a Bf109 of JG27 south of the Needles during the afternoon of 20 July. The son of an Italian father, de Mancha was twenty-three years old and had only just completed training before he joined No. 43 Squadron just two weeks earlier. His body was never found and he is also remembered on the Runnymede Memorial. It had been a bad start to the battle for No. 43 Squadron and Tangmere. The squadron detached to Northolt on 23 July for a rest but returned to Tangmere one week later.

By the beginning of August the satellite airfield at nearby Westhampnett was ready for operations and No. 145 Squadron left Tangmere and moved in to the new airfield.

A particularly busy day for Tangmere was 8 August, when more than 100 sorties were flown between the three squadrons during the day. During the late afternoon Nos 43 and 601 Squadrons were heavily involved in the air battle over Convoy CW9, code-named 'Peewit', as it passed through the Channel. No. 43 became engaged with Ju87s and Bf109s, which resulted in the loss of two Hurricanes and both pilots. One of the pilots who added to his total during the action was Pilot Officer Tony Woods-Scawen, who destroyed a Bf110 of LG1 south of the Isle of Wight. He then attacked a formation of about fifty Ju87s and his aircraft was hit by return fire from another Bf110 but he managed to return to base. At twenty-two years old, Tony Woods-Scawen was the younger of two brothers. Both he and his elder brother, Patrick, served with Fighter Command during the Battle of Britain. Both became aces and both were awarded the DFC. Tragically, however, both were killed during the battle. Tony was killed on 2 September whilst serving at Tangmere, shot down in flames during combat with Bf109s over east Kent. Although he managed to bale out he was too low for his parachute to save him. Tragically for the Woods-Scawen family, he was killed just twenty-four hours after Patrick had died in similar circumstances whilst serving with No. 85 Squadron at Croydon. Tony is buried in Folkestone New Cemetery in Kent and Patrick in Caterham and Warlingham Burial Ground in Surrey.

During the morning of 11 August, Tangmere suffered further losses when four Hurricanes of No. 601 Squadron were shot down during one engagement, with all four pilots killed. The twelve Hurricanes were led by Flight Lieutenant William Rhodes-Moorhouse, the only son of the first winner of the Victoria Cross for air operations, and the squadron intercepted a large formation of enemy aircraft off Portland at 20,000 ft. During the encounter Rhodes-Moorhouse claimed two Bf109s south of Swanage but one of the squadron pilots killed was his brother-in-law, 21-year-old Flying Officer Richard Demetriadi, who was last seen chasing an enemy aircraft across the Channel. An initial search found nothing but his body was eventually recovered and he was buried in France. In memory of his son, Sir Stephen Demetriadi gave land at Ditchling Beacon, high on the South Downs north of Brighton, to the National Trust. Sadly, William Rhodes-Moorhouse was later killed whilst also operating from Tangmere. During combat over Tunbridge Wells on 6 September, he was shot down and his Hurricane crashed at Southborough. He is buried in the private cemetery at the family home at Beaminster in Dorset.

Spitfires of No. 266 Squadron arrived at Tangmere to replace the Hurricanes of No. 1 Squadron, which had moved to Northolt on 1 August. The new arrivals were soon in action on 12 August when they intercepted a large formation of Ju88s attacking Portsmouth. Two were shot down, with the loss of Pilot Officer Dennis Ashton. The Spitfires left Tangmere the same day but it had been another busy day for the station with all four squadrons involved and, once again, more than 100 sorties were flown from the airfield during the day.

As the *Luftwaffe* turned its attention to the airfields of Fighter Command, Tangmere came under heavy attack at 1.00 p.m. on 16 August. Both Hurricane squadrons were airborne to protect the airfield but they could do little to prevent the attack and the result was devastating. Two hangars were completely destroyed and the other three were left badly damaged. Many of the station's technical and domestic buildings were also completely destroyed and it was left without water and sanitation. There was also considerable damage to a number of aircraft that had been caught on the ground during the attack. All of the Blenheims belonging to the FIU had been destroyed or badly damaged and four Hurricanes of No. 43 Squadron were completely destroyed. Thirteen of the station's personnel, including three civilians, were killed and twenty more injured.

Following the attack, a Hurricane of No. 601 Squadron landed back at Tangmere having been badly damaged during an attack on a Ju87. The pilot was a wealthy young American volunteer, Pilot Officer Billy Fiske, who was also a keen sportsman and had captained the winning

US Olympic bobsled team in 1932. At the outbreak of the Second World War, the US authorities made it difficult for Americans to volunteer for service in Britain, but Billy Fiske used his connections to volunteer for the RAF and joined No. 601 Squadron at Tangmere in July 1940. Although he managed to force land his damaged aircraft back at Tangmere he was badly burned and admitted to hospital, but died of his injuries the following day. He was twenty-nine years old. On 4 July 1941, American Independence Day, a bronze plaque was unveiled in St Paul's Cathedral by the Secretary of State for Air, Sir Archibald Sinclair. Billy Fiske is buried in Saints Mary and Blaise churchyard in Boxgrove near the village of Tangmere.

There was, however, some success for the Tangmere squadrons during the action of 16 August, with seven Ju87s and two Bf109s claimed as destroyed. Two of the Ju87s were destroyed by Sergeant Leonard Guy, one reportedly forced into the sea despite Guy being out of ammunition. Nevertheless, it had generally been a bad day for Tangmere.

Despite the damage caused on 16 August, Tangmere remained operational but it was necessary to disperse many of the station's personnel. The operations room was moved to St James' School in Chichester and Shopwyke House near Goodwood temporarily became the officers mess. The FIU's only remaining serviceable aircraft, a Beaufighter, was moved to Shoreham and blast pens were constructed at Tangmere to help protect the remaining fighters.

No. 601 Squadron suffered further losses on 18 August when Bf109s of JG27 shot down two of its Hurricanes off the Sussex coast during the afternoon; both pilots were killed. The following day, it exchanged places with No. 17 Squadron at Debden but returned to Tangmere on 2 September, and No. 17 moved back to Debden. During the morning of 6 September No. 601 lost four Hurricanes during an engagement with Bf109s over Mayfield. Tragically for the squadron, both of the flight commanders were killed; one was William Rhodes-Moorhouse as previously described, and the other was the American Flying Officer Carl Davis, who had been with the squadron since the outbreak of the war. Davis had just been awarded the DFC for the destruction of nine enemy aircraft, all whilst serving at Tangmere. His Hurricane crashed near Tunbridge Wells.

The loss of four more Hurricanes and two of its most experienced pilots resulted in No. 601 Squadron being withdrawn to Exeter the following day for a rest, being replaced by No. 213 Squadrons. There was a further change when No. 43 Squadron left Tangmere on 8

September, having been replaced by No. 607 Squadron. This squadron had been heavily involved in the Battle of France during May 1940, and claimed seventy enemy aircraft destroyed during eleven days of fighting. Its introduction to the Battle of Britain, however, proved disastrous. During the late afternoon of 9 September it intercepted a large formation of Do17s escorted by Bf109s over Mayfield. Five of its Hurricanes were shot down and a sixth force landed near Knockholt; three pilots were killed. One aircraft, flown by Pilot Officer Stuart Parnall, crashed at Goudhurst and a second, flown by Pilot Officer John Lenahan, at Cranbrook. The third pilot to die was Pilot Officer George Drake, who also crashed at Goudhurst. Drake was South African and had made his way to England, where he had volunteered for the RAF just before the outbreak of war. He had celebrated his twentieth birthday just six weeks before his death. His Hurricane was eventually excavated in 1972 and Drake was buried with full military honours at Brookwood Military Cemetery.

On 12 September Wing Commander John Dewar failed to arrive at Tangmere following a routine transit flight from Exeter. Dewar had commanded No. 87 Squadron during the Battle of France and had been awarded the DSO and DFC for his leadership and destruction of five enemy aircraft. His body was eventually washed up along the Sussex coast and is buried in St John the Baptist churchyard at North Baddesley in Hampshire.

No. 607 Squadron lost five pilots during one week at the end of September and begining of October. This brought the

John Dewar commanded No. 87 Squadron in France and was one of the first four officers to receive the double award of the DSO and DFC. On 12 September 1940 he failed to arrive at Tangmere following a transit from Exeter.

The grave of John Dewar in St John the Baptist churchyard in North Baddesley, Hampshire.

squadron's period at Tangmere to a close and it moved to Scotland on 10 October. It was replaced by No. 145 Squadron, which returned to Tangmere for its second period of operations during the battle.

The last casualty from Tangmere during the Battle of Britain was Pilot Officer Richard Hutley of No. 213 Squadron, who was shot down off Selsey on 29 October. He managed to bale out but was found dead when picked up. He was just twenty-two years old and is buried in St Andrew's churchyard at Tangmere.

Tangmere was used by a number of different aircraft and units after the Battle of Britain. Some of the more interesting residents included the Special Duty units, which were used to ferry Special Operations Executive (SOE) agents into occupied France. The airfield was extended during 1941–2 and several improvements were made. Two asphalt runways were constructed, the longest nearly 2,000 yards. During 1942 and 1943 several different squadrons used Tangmere for carrying out offensive operations over France. With the increase in the bomber offensive, the airfield's long and hardened runways proved useful to damaged aircraft returning back from operations across the Channel. In June 1944 it was used extensively during the D-Day operations but the number of operations from the airfield reduced as the Allied advance into Europe increased.

After the Second World War the airfield was refurbished in preparation for the RAF's new jet fighters and became home to Meteor fighters during the 1950s. It was transferred to Signals Command in 1958 and was used by Canberras and Varsities before being transferred to Transport Command in 1963 as a non-flying support unit. Following a brief period under the new Support Command, it closed in 1970.

The history of the famous airfield a Tangmere has lived on through the Military Aviation Museum.

Although some of the wartime hangars remained, most of the buildings were demolished during the early 1980s as some of the land was developed for housing and business. The site today is a mixture of agriculture, housing and business. There are some reminders of the former airfield but these are not accessible to the public. However, the history of this former Battle of Britain airfield has been preserved by the Tangmere Military Aviation Museum, which first opened in 1982. It is located 3 miles to the east of Chichester, just south of the A27 in Tangmere Road, in one of the original radio repair huts on the edge of the former airfield. It is well signposted from the A27. The museum is maintained by a group of dedicated volunteers as a lasting tribute to the men and women who served the cause of freedom and covers the history of Tangmere airfield and the Battle of Britain. It is open daily from February to November but is closed in December and January. The opening times are: February from 10.00 a.m. to 4.30 p.m., March to October from 10.00 a.m. to 5.30 p.m., and November from 10.00 a.m. to 4.30 p.m. Admission is £5.00 for adults, £1.50 for children, £4.00 for Seniors and £11.00 for a family of two adults and two children. There are reduced rates for school parties or pre-arranged bookings for a minimum of twelve persons. There are good amenities at the museum with car parking, a café, souvenir shop and toilets. There is also access for the disabled. The address is: Tangmere Airfield, Chichester, West Sussex, PO20 6ES. Telephone: 01243 775223. Fax: 01243 789490.

Other places of interest in and around Tangmere village include the Bader Arms, less than ten minutes walk from the museum, and a small memorial stone in the village, which was erected by the locals in 1976 near St Andrew's Church. In the churchyard are the graves of airmen

The tail of a Lightning is just visible as it stands proudly outside the Military Aviation Museum and alongside the former airfield.

killed during the war, including as already mentioned, Pilot Officer Richard Hutley, the last Tangmere pilot killed during the Battle of Britain.

Squadron	From	To	Aircraft	Sqn Code
145 Sqn	Start (10/5/40) 9/10/40	31/7/40 End (7/5/41)	Hurricane	SO
43 Sqn	Start (31/5/40) 1/8/40	23/7/40 8/9/40	Hurricane	NQ
601 Sqn	Start 17/6/40 2/9/40	19/8/40 7/9/40	Hurricane	UF
1 Sqn	Start 23/6/40	1/8/40	Hurricane	JX
266 Sqn	9/8/40	12/8/40	Spitfire	UO
17 Sqn	19/8/40	2/9/40	Hurricane	YB
607 Sqn	1/9/40	10/10/40	Hurricane	AF
213 Sqn	7/9/40	End (29/11/40)	Hurricane	AK
FIU	Start (18/4/40)	20/8/40	Blenheim	

Summary of Squadrons at Tangmere

Westhampnett

Now known as Goodwood Airfield, the former airfield of Westhampnett is situated less than 2 miles to the north-east of Chichester and was developed just before the Second World War when the Air Ministry needed more airfields. A large area of open land within the Goodwood Estate of the Duke of Richmond and Gordon was considered suitable as an emergency landing ground for fighters based at Tangmere. At first the land was maintained as an open area available for emergency landings only, and it remained that way until the Germans invaded France and the Low Countries during May 1940. Westhampnett was then upgraded to satellite status and by the start of the Battle of Britain it was being used as a landing ground for the Hurricanes based at Tangmere.

The airfield had four grass runways, with the longest (south-east – north-west) being 1,500 yards. The second (south-west – north-east) was 1,100 yards, the third (north-south) 1,000 yards and the fourth (east-west) 900 yards. Initially, accommodation was basic to say the least and consisted of bell tents with no messing facilities at all. Aircraft were dispersed around the airfield and serviced in blister hangars, and there was a basic watch tower in the north-east corner of the airfield. The limited facilities meant that only one squadron at a time could operate from Westhampnett during the Battle of Britain, and it was only home to two squadrons during the entire battle.

No. 145 Squadron moved to Westhampnett on 31 July as the first resident squadron, although one of its pilots had already made use of the airfield the week before when Pilot Officer Jas Storrar crash-landed his Hurricane on 24 July. It was his nineteenth birthday but he was already an ace with five confirmed kills and was one of the finest to fly from Westhampnett during the early weeks of the battle; he went on to be credited with twelve confirmed kills.

On the day after the squadron moved in one of its Hurricanes was lost whilst attacking a Henschel Hs126 about 10 miles to the south of Hastings. Although the Henschel was shot down, the Hurricane was hit by return fire and the pilot, Sub-Lieutenant Ian Kestin, crashed into the Channel and became the first casualty from Westhampnett during the battle. He is remembered on the Fleet Air Arm Memorial at Lee-on-Solent.

Westhampnett was one of No. 11 Group's most southerly airfields, which meant that reaction time was often short. Within a matter of days the squadron had seen considerable action, having flown virtually every day during early August in defence of the convoys operating in the Channel and to intercept enemy formations. The heaviest combat took place on 8 August when the squadron claimed eleven kills but lost five Hurricanes. In the morning the squadron was in action with Bf109s of JG27 to the south of the Isle of Wight; two Hurricanes were shot down with both pilots missing. Later that afternoon it was protecting Convoy CW9, code-named 'Peewit', in its attempt to pass through the Dover Straits.

One of the successful Westhampnett pilots that day was Pilot Officer Archibald Weir, who was credited with three kills and won a DFC. Weir was later shot down and killed off the Isle of Wight on 7 November, the first of three tragedies for the Weir family. His father, a serving RAF officer, was killed in 1941, when the ship he was in was torpedoed and sunk, and his younger brother was killed at Anzio in 1944. The squadron lost three more Hurricanes during the final engagement of the day. All three pilots were missing: Pilot Officer Ernest Wakeham was last seen engaging Ju87s and Bf110s, Sub-Lieutenant Francis Smith was seen to crash into the sea and Flying Officer the Lord Richard Kay-Shuttleworth was last seen in combat with Ju87s and Bf110s above the convoy to the south of the Isle of Wight. A descendant of this famous family, Lord Shuttleworth is remembered on the Runnymede Memorial. The day marked the end of the first week of operations from the new airfield. There was a visit from HRH the Duke of Gloucester and telegrams of congratulations from various senior officers to celebrate the success. However, the loss of five pilots in one day was a tragic blow.

The squadron was involved in further heavy fighting just three days later, on 11 August, during a patrol between Portland and Swanage, when it intercepted a force of more than 100 enemy aircraft heading towards the naval base. On the following day, it was once again in action when it intercepted a formation of 150 aircraft, consisting of Ju88s of KG51 escorted by Bf109s of JG53 and Bf110s of ZG2 and ZG76, attacking the Royal Navy base at Portsmouth. One successful pilot on the day was the Pole, Flying Officer Witold Urbanowicz, who had joined the squadron at Westhampnett just the week before. He had destroyed a Bf110 on 8 August and now claimed a Ju88 south of the Isle of Wight. These were the first two of his fifteen confirmed kills during the Battle of Britain. However, three more Hurricanes failed to return to Westhampnett; all three pilots were missing. Pilot Officer John Harrison and Sergeant Josef Kwiecinski had only joined the squadron at Westhampnett the week before. Another Polish pilot, Flight Lieutenant Wilhelm Pankratz was also reported missing after engaging the enemy south of the Isle of Wight. Both of the Poles are commemorated on the Polish Air Force Memorial at Northolt and John Harrison on the Runnymede Memorial.

These losses were as much as any squadron could be expected to take. Although Westhampnett had been involved in operations for just twelve days, No. 145 Squadron had already lost eleven Hurricanes and eleven pilots had been killed – ten in just five days. It had been a hard beginning for those at Westhampnett and it was no surprise when the squadron was moved north to Scotland on 13 August for a rest. There were just four pilots left.

Moving south to replace the Hurricanes were the Spitfires of No. 602 'City of Glasgow' Squadron, which arrived at Westhampnett the following day. The newcomers were soon in action and scored their first victory early on 15 August with the destruction of a long-range reconnaissance Dornier Do17P off the Isle of Wight. The squadron experienced its first combat the following afternoon, when Tangmere came under heavy attack from Ju87s escorted by Bf109s. Later in the afternoon the squadron carried out a coastal patrol, during which they claimed the destruction of two Bf110s of ZG76, one of which crashed into the grounds at Shopwhyke Hall near Tangmere, where the old mansion on the estate was used by the resident squadron at Westhampnett.

Two days later the squadron was again in action, this time protecting targets along the south coast including the airfields of Ford, Gosport and Thorney Island, as well as the radar site at Poling. It was heavily involved with Ju87s and Bf109s over Ford and a number of Spitfires were damaged. It claimed four enemy aircraft destroyed. Two credited to Sergeant Basil Whall, both Ju87s of StG77; he shot one down into the sea and the other managed to force-land on a golf course at Littlehampton. Whall had been hit by return fire during the engagement and had to ditch at Elmer Sands, Middleton, but was unhurt. He was one of No. 602 Squadron's most successful pilots at Westhampnett; six of his seven confirmed kills were achieved whilst operating from the airfield. Sadly he was not to survive the battle and died in hospital after crashing following damage by a Ju88 on 7 October. He was twenty-two years old.

On 24 August the *Luftwaffe* turned its attention to the destruction of Fighter Command's airfields but Westhampnett survived any major attack. No. 602 Squadron did, however, play its part during the vital defence of No. 11 Group's airfields. It lost two Spitfires on 25 August over Dorchester and Portland, and was in action again the following day with Bf109s of JG53 over Selsey Bill. Two Spitfires failed to return to Westhampnett; one crash landed at Tangmere and the other, flown by Sergeant Cyril Babbage, who had already claimed a Bf109 earlier in the combat, was shot down into the sea. He managed to bale out unhurt. He was another successful sergeant pilot at Westhampnett, being credited with seven kills, for which he was awarded the DFM and later commissioned before he left Westhampnett at the end of the battle.

The *Luftwaffe* tactics changed on 7 September, when it began bombing London. There followed a gradual reduction in the intensity of operations from Westhampnett, as it was the furthest west of all No.

A Spitfire of No. 602 Squadron lands back at Westhampnett during September 1940.

11 Group's airfields. As the *Luftwaffe* began bombing London by night, some of No. 602 Squadron took part in night flying practice from Tangmere on 10 September. However, the Spitfire proved unsuitable for night operations and night flying soon came to an end after three aircraft were damaged during landing, one of which crash-landed at Felpham Golf Course.

During the rest of September Westhampnett lost just one more pilot, during an engagement with Bf110s south of Selsey Bill during the late afternoon of 11 September. The pilot was Sergeant Mervyn Sprague, whose body was washed ashore at Brighton a month later. He is buried in St Andrews churchyard at Tangmere.

The remaining period of the Battle of Britain was relatively quiet for No. 602 Squadron although there was, of course, the sad loss of Basil Whall on 7 October. The only further casualty during the battle was Sergeant Douglas Elcombe, who failed to return to Westhampnett on 26 October from a routine midday patrol. The circumstances of his death are unknown and he is commemorated on the Runnymede Memorial.

With the battle over, the Spitfires of No. 602 Squadron returned to Scotland. Westhampnett was then home to various RAF fighter squadrons for a variety of roles, such as offensive sweeps across the Channel and convoy patrols. In August 1942 the airfield became USAAF Station 352. During 1943 it was developed to include a tarmac perimeter track, and the shortest runway was extended to just over 1,000 yards. The accommodation was also improved by the addition of Nissen huts. In April 1944 three Canadian Spitfire squadrons operated briefly from Westhampnett before the commencement of D-Day operations. However, the airfield was not considered particularly suitable as a forward operating base to support the advance from Normandy during the summer of 1944. It was of grass and was difficult to operate from when wet; it had always suffered from water logging following any period of heavy rain. It therefore, had limited use as the advance into Europe continued.

Westhampnett was put on care and maintenance in January 1945 and was transferred from No. 11 Group to Supreme Headquarters, Allied Expeditionary Forces (SHAEF) as a rear headquarters. The airfield did reopen briefly after the end of hostilities but was placed on care and maintenance once again before it closed in 1946.

As a motor-racing enthusiast, the Duke of Richmond and Gordon noted that the airfield facilities offered potential as a racing circuit, in particular by making use of the tarmac perimeter track, and the site was renamed and became home to the Goodwood Motor Racing Circuit in September 1948. As racing cars became faster the track became increasingly dangerous and the cost of providing all the safety features required was considered too high, so racing ceased in 1965. The site was resurrected as an airfield and developed by the Goodwood Terrena Company, which made use of the old RAF facilities, combined with a new hangar and new flying club accommodation.

The airfield is part of the Goodwood complex and remains active as a flying club. With three grass runways and thousands of aircraft movements each year, it is ideally situated for civil light aviation and is set within 12,000 acres of beautiful countryside, which also includes the motor-racing circuit and a horse-racing course. The airfield offers flying instruction and a base for private aircraft. Some of the former RAF buildings such as the large sheds and old air traffic control tower remain. It can be reached by taking the A27 out of Chichester towards Worthing; Goodwood is soon signposted off a large roundabout. Follow the signs for the aerodrome and the motor circuit is reached on the left. Entrance to the aerodrome is through the underpass, which is only big enough for cars. The address is: Goodwood Airfield, Goodwood, Chichester, West Sussex, PO18 0PH. Tel: 01243 755061.

Squadron	From	To	Aircraft	Sqn Code
145 Sqn	31/7/40	13/8/40	Hurricane	SO
602 Sqn	14/8/40	End (17/12/40)	Spitfire	LO

Summary of Squadrons at Westhampnett

The former airfield of Westhampnett is now an active flying club within the complex of the Goodwood Motor Circuit.

Shoreham

One mile west of Shoreham-by-Sea in West Sussex, Shoreham airfield was first developed as early as 1911. When the Germans advanced through France and the Low Countries in May 1940, the Air Ministry took over Shoreham as an advanced operating airfield for No. 11 Group. Initially it was only used by No. 225 Squadron, which operated Lysanders for coastal patrols. There was no accommodation at the airfield and so a nearby hotel became the officers' mess and a local engineering firm provided accommodation for the sergeant pilots, whilst the other non-commissioned officers and airmen were accommodated by local families. On 20 August the FIU moved into Shoreham with just one Blenheim, the unit's only surviving aircraft following an attack on its previous base at Tangmere four days earlier. The unit then took delivery of a Beaufighter night-fighter and this aircraft flew the FIU's first operational sortie on 4/5 September. The following week the unit suffered its only operational loss during the Battle of Britain when its Blenheim failed to return to Shoreham following a night patrol off Calais, although the circumstances of the loss are unknown; the crew of three baled out and were taken prisoner. No. 422 Flight moved to Shoreham on 14 October and was equipped with Hurricanes, which also flew in the night-fighter role. It is now a municipal airport and is situated alongside the A27 Brighton to Worthing Road.

Ford

Located 2 miles to the west of Littlehampton, Ford was a Royal Navy airfield during most of the Battle of Britain but was transferred to No. 11 Group towards the end of the battle. The airfield was first developed in 1917 and was originally known as Ford Junction or Yapton. It became RAF Ford in 1937, as part of Coastal Command, before it was transferred to the Admiralty in May 1939 and commissioned as HMS *Peregrine*. A number of naval squadrons used it during the opening months of the Second World War but it was only used by training units during the opening period of the Battle of Britain.

The Germans believed that it was one of No. 11 Group's main fighter bases and attacked it during the early afternoon of 18 August. As it was not actually being used by No. 11 Group at that time, it was not protected by fighters and the thirty Ju87s of StG77 met no opposition. The attack proved devastating and several aircraft on the ground were destroyed. There were also direct hits on hangars, fuel installations and several technical and domestic buildings. Twenty-eight personnel were killed and dozens more wounded. As the Ju87s tried to make their escape, however, Spitfires of No. 602 Squadron from nearby Westhampnett intercepted them and shot down three before they, in turn, were attacked by the escorting Bf109s of JG27.

Blenheims of No. 23 Squadron moved into Ford on 12 September and operated in the night-fighter role. The airfield was transferred back to the RAF on 1 October and was part of No. 11 Group for the remainder of the Battle of Britain. There were four raids on it during October but they caused no significant damage.

At the end of the war Ford was transferred back to the Admiralty as HMS *Peregrine* once more. In 1958 it was closed and the site was transferred to the Home Office as an open prison, although part of the site was used for flying until 1980. The site of the former airfield is between the village of Ford and the A259, and is now used by HMP Ford, which is a Category D training establishment.

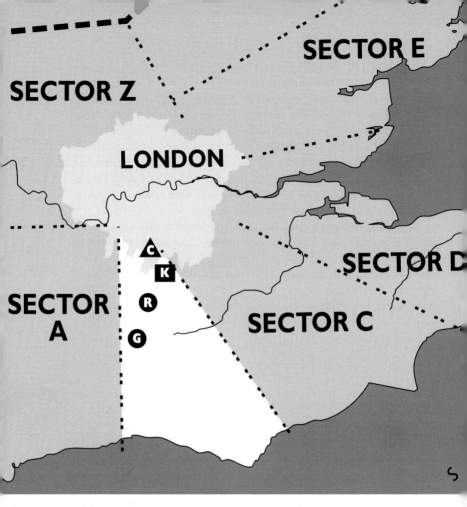

SECTOR B – AUGUST 1940

KEY:-

K = Kenley, Sector Airfield

C = Croydon, Satellite Airfield

R = Redhill, Emergency Satellite

G = Gatwick, Emergency Satellite

CHAPTER FOUR

KENLEY SECTOR
SECTOR B

East of the Tangmere Sector was the Kenley Sector, or Sector B. Kenley's area of responsibility was from the boundary of Sector A, for a short distance along the southern edge of London to Croydon and then south-east to a point between Eastbourne and Hastings on the coast. The areas within the sector that were of greatest interest to the *Luftwaffe* were the two main airfields of No. 11 Group and their satellites, and the radar sites at Pevensey, Beachy Head and Truleigh near Brighton. The two main airfields were the sector airfield of Kenley itself and its satellite airfield at Croydon. No. 11 Group also used two other airfields, at Redhill and Gatwick, as emergency satellites and these airfields are briefly covered.

Kenley

Kenley airfield was developed on land on Kenley Common to the south of Croydon in Surrey. It first opened in 1917 and was used as an aircraft acceptance park in preparation for the delivery of aircraft to operational units in France. When the First World War ended all the units moved out but because of its facilities the RAF retained it as a permanent station. Kenley's first post-war resident squadron was No. 24 Squadron, which reformed at Kenley in April 1920 as a communications and training squadron. It operated several different types during its seven years at Kenley, primarily providing air transport for the Government as well as maintaining a flight of aircraft for training.

No. 32 Squadron also served at Kenley between 1923 and 1932, during which time No. 24 Squadron was replaced by No. 23. One famous incident occurred during this period when Douglas Bader, who was based at Kenley, clipped the ground whilst practising low level aerobatics in a Bulldog at Woodley aerodrome in December 1931. Although he survived the crash he lost both his legs but went on to become a legend during the Second World War.

Both Nos 23 and 32 Squadrons left Kenley in September 1932 so that reconstruction could take place. Work was completed in 1934 and Nos 3 and 17 Squadrons arrived that May. Both squadrons remained at

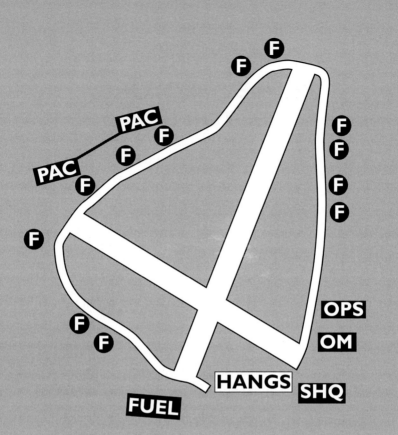

KENLEY – AUGUST 1940

KEY:-

F = Fighter Dispersals

OPS = Sector Operations Room

OM = Officers Mess

HANGS = Hangers

SHQ = Station Headquarters

FUEL = Fuel Dump

PAC = Line of Parachute and Cable Installations

Kenley until 1939, when Nos 46 and 615 Squadrons arrived. During the final months before the Second World War there were several movements and the airfield went through more construction work, which included two runways (1,000 yards and 1,200 yards) and twelve concrete aircraft pens.

Kenley was established as the sector airfield for Sector B of No. 11 Group. When the Battle of Britain opened the airfield was home to the Spitfires of No. 64 Squadron and the Hurricanes of No. 615 Squadron, which had both moved in during May. It was one of Fighter Command's most vital airfields, and together with Biggin Hill covered the approaches to London from the south and south-east.

The Kenley squadrons were in action during the opening days of the battle. The first casualty was Pilot Officer Michael Mudie, a Hurricane pilot serving with No. 615 Squadron. He was taking part in a convoy patrol during the afternoon of 14 July when Bf109s of JG51 shot him down off Dover. Mudie managed to bale out and was picked up by the Royal Navy and admitted to Dover Hospital but died of his injuries the following day.

The first pilot from No. 64 Squadron to be killed whilst operating from Kenley during the battle was twenty-two-year-old Flying Officer Alistair Jeffrey, who was shot down off Dover during the afternoon of 25 July. His Spitfire was one of two lost by the squadron off the south coast. His body was eventually washed ashore in Holland.

The first two weeks of August were hectic, particularly for Kenley's Spitfires. No. 64 Squadron was taken by surprise on a patrol over the Channel during the early morning of 5 August and one aircraft, flown by Sergeant Lewis Isaac, failed to return. There was a further loss just three days later when Pilot Officer Peter Kennard-Davis was shot down during combat with Bf109s of JG51 to the north of Dover soon after midday on 8 August. He managed to bale out but was badly wounded. He was admitted to the Royal Victoria Hospital but died two days later. No. 615 Squadron also suffered losses during early August. Two Hurricanes were lost during the early afternoon of 14 August when the squadron intercepted Bf110s over Dover; both pilots were killed. The activity from Kenley during this period peaked on 15 August when the three squadrons flew nearly 100 sorties between them.

The first attack on Kenley airfield took place at 1.15 p.m. on 18 August. It was attacked from both medium and low level by about fifty Do17s of KG76 escorted by Bf109s. It suffered considerable damage as more than 100 bombs landed on the airfield. Three Hurricanes of No. 615 Squadron were destroyed on the ground and three hangars,

Above: The same part of the airfield today alongside Hayes Lane where the 'Tribute to Kenley' memorial has been erected.

Right: A Spitfire of No. 64 Squadron in a blast pen at Kenley during a low level attack by Do17s of KG76 on 18 August.

plus a number of other buildings, were also destroyed. Damage was also caused to several other hangars and the vital operations room had been put out of action. There was considerable damage to other aircraft on the ground, as well as to the water and gas supplies. Nine of the station's personnel were killed during the raid and a further ten were injured. Fortunately, the duty controller took the initiative to scramble the fighters when he realized an attack was inevitable, and this undoubtedly prevented further losses. Of the Hurricanes that did get airborne five were shot down or severely damaged by the attacking Bf109s. One, flown by the Canadian Flight Lieutenant Lionel Gaunce, crashed at Sevenoaks Weald; Gaunce baled out and was admitted to hospital. A second, flown by the South African Pilot Officer Petrus Hugo, managed to crash land at Orpington; Hugo survived and was admitted to hospital. A third managed to force land back at Kenley. Another was shot down in flames and crashed on Morden Park Golf Course; Sergeant Peter Walley was killed. He was just twenty years old and is buried in St.Luke's churchyard at Whyteleafe. The fifth aircraft was attempting a forced landing back at Kenley after the action but was further damaged when it was shot at by the airfield defences; fortunately, Pilot Officer David Looker survived and was admitted to Croydon Hospital with severe shock and concussion.

It had been a disastrous day for Kenley. The only good thing was that many of the bombs dropped from a very low height had failed to explode. This was probably due to the airfield's anti-aircraft defences, which were credited with bringing down a Do17 of KG76 during the attack. The Dornier crashed in flames at Golf Road, just outside the airfield boundary and came down on a private house. Miraculously the owner survived, although the house was destroyed. The Dornier's crew of four and an official German war correspondent on board were all killed. In addition to the Dornier brought down, a second had also been hit by Kenley's defences and crashed near Biggin Hill; the crew were captured.

The following day No. 64 Squadron was replaced by No. 616, which was in action almost immediately. It lost two pilots within a few days when their Spitfires failed to return following combat with Bf109s over Canterbury during the early evening of 25 August. Both Kenley squadrons also suffered losses during the afternoon of 26 August. No. 615 Squadron lost four Spitfires during two separate actions with Bf109s and in another action with Bf109s off Dover just after midday, No. 616 Squadron lost five Spitfires. It had been another bad day for Kenley.

No. 615 Squadron was replaced by No. 253, which was equipped with Hurricanes, on 29 August, and No. 616 left on 2 September. During its short stay of two weeks it had suffered badly. In just six days at the end of August it had lost four pilots with four more wounded and one taken prisoner.

No. 253 Squadron suffered a disastrous start at Kenley. By the end of its first full day of operations on 30 August it had lost five Hurricanes in two separate actions, one with Bf109s over Redhill in the morning and the other with Bf109s over Dungeness in the afternoon. Three pilots were killed. Pilot Officer Colin Francis was just nineteen years old and Pilot Officer David Jenkins and Sergeant John Dickinson were both twenty-one.

There was a further loss for the squadron on the following day when the commanding officer, Squadron Leader Harold Starr, was shot down during a morning patrol. Although he managed to bale out, he fell dead in his parachute near Eastry in Kent. Command of the squadron was passed to Squadron Leader Tom Gleave, but he too was

Myles Duke-Woolley was promoted to the rank of Squadron Leader on 27 September and took command of No. 253 Sqn at Kenley. He was the squadron's fifth CO in a month.

shot down later in the day when attacking Ju88s. He survived but was badly burned and was admitted to hospital. On 6 September the new acting commanding officer, Squadron Leader William Cambridge, crashed near Ashford in Kent during a routine morning patrol. The squadron had lost three commanding officers in a week. Command was then given to Squadron Leader Gerald Edge, who was posted in to the squadron. Edge had already enjoyed much success with No. 605 Squadron with seven confirmed kills and had been awarded the DFC. He went on to become one of Kenley's most successful fighter pilots. During his first full day in command he destroyed two He111s over Thameshaven. This was followed on 9 September by the destruction of four Ju88s to the north-east of London, and on 11 September he destroyed two He111s and a Bf109. His luck, however, ran out on 26 September when he was shot down and admitted to Ashford Hospital. Command of the squadron was then passed to Squadron Leader Myles Duke-Woolley, who remained in command until the end of the battle.

Kenley suffered a further attack from medium level on 1 September. Just one bomb landed within the airfield boundary, with the others falling in the local vicinity. There were no reported casualties.

No. 66 Squadron replaced No. 616 on 3 September but remained at Kenley for just a week. On 4 September it lost three Spitfires over Ashford and a further two on the following day. Short as it was, it was a bad stay for No. 66 Squadron. There were, however, some notable successes during early September. On the 4th, for example, No. 253 Squadron claimed six Bf110s for the loss of just one Hurricane.

No. 501 Squadron, equipped with Hurricanes, arrived at Kenley on 10 September and remained for the rest of the battle. On 13 September Sergeant James 'Ginger' Lacey was hit by return fire from an He111 over Maidstone and had to bale out. Lacey had taken off from Kenley alone and had been stalking the Heinkel, which had reportedly bombed Buckingham Palace, for some time in and out of cloud before he shot it down. It was his sixteenth kill of the war and his eleventh during the battle. Born in Yorkshire, Lacey joined the RAF Voluntary Reserve (RAFVR) in 1937 and was posted to No. 501 Squadron as a sergeant pilot. During the Battle of France he destroyed five aircraft. By the time he arrived at Kenley he had increased his total to fifteen destroyed and had been awarded the DFM. He destroyed a further three aircraft on 15 September: two Bf109s and an He111. On 27 September he added a further Bf109 to his total and he was undoubtedly one of the finest to have flown from Kenley during the Battle of Britain.

Both Kenley squadrons suffered further losses during October and there were several attacks against the airfield before the end of the battle. In one particular attack during the early evening of 17 October a number of aircraft on the ground were hit and two station personnel were killed. The last pilot to die whilst operating from Kenley during the battle was Pilot Officer Vilem Goth, a Czech pilot serving with No. 501 Squadron. He was killed on 25 October when he collided with another squadron aircraft during combat with Bf109s over Tenterden; the other pilot baled out unhurt. Despite the losses, there were notable successes during the final weeks of the battle. 'Ginger' Lacey brought his total to twenty-three confirmed destroyed, for which he was awarded a bar to his DFM. This made him the RAF's top-scoring ace of the Battle of Britain.

By early 1941 Hurricanes of Nos 1 and 615 Squadrons had moved into Kenley to replace both Nos 253 and 501. Both squadrons were involved in offensive operations in northern France. Spitfires replaced the Hurricanes during the latter half of 1941, and by the end of the following year the airfield was home to the Canadian Wing. It played host to various Canadian squadrons for much of the next two years. Its tasks were taken over by Biggin Hill in March 1944 and it was closed to flying during the summer when the V-1 rockets were launched against London.

After the Second World War Kenley was transferred to Transport Command and then to Reserve Command. For a short period during the late 1940s a passenger service was operated from the airfield. During the 1950s it was used by auxiliary air observation flights and also became a star in various film sets, including *Angels One Five* (1951) and *Reach for the Sky* (1955). RAF Kenley closed in May 1959 but the airfield remained in use for gliding until it was finally placed on care and maintenance in 1966. The air traffic control tower and some of the hangars were demolished in 1978 following a fire.

The airfield is still used for gliding. The resident users are the

Surrey Hill Gliding Club and the appropriately numbered No. 615 Volunteer Gliding School (VGS), which provides gliding for the air cadets and Combined Cadet Forces of Surrey, Sussex, Kent and London. It is also home to No. 450 (Kenley) Squadron of the ATC. Although most of the land is still owned by the Ministry of Defence, much of it is available to the public as Kenley Common. The airfield is situated between the A22 (to its east) and the B2030 (to its south and west) but is not particularly easy to find, and could easily be missed when driving south on the A22 from Croydon towards Caterham. The best way to find it from the A23 London to Brighton road, is to take the A22 at Purley (south of Croydon) towards Caterham, then proceed through the village of Kenley and turn right at the roundabout at the village of Whyteleafe, towards the railway station. Continue along the road, crossing the railway line, and proceed up Whyteleafe Hill with St Luke's Church on the left. At the top of the hill turn right. This is the southern part of the airfield, which is used by the Surrey Gliding Club and No. 615 VGS. Some former buildings remain, including the officers' and sergeants' messes, and the local RAF Association meets in one of the airfield's former administration buildings.

Continuing along the road around the western side of the airfield, there is a 'Tribute to Kenley' memorial. It cannot be seen from the road, as it is situated in one of the former aircraft blast pens, although it is signposted from the road. It can be reached by parking the car and entering Kenley Common, and then walking a few yards along the footpath. On leaving the memorial continue along the road, with the airfield on the right, turn left from Hayes Lane into Old Lodge Lane and you will reach the Wattenden Arms. This was a favourite pub of those serving at Kenley and there are several pictures and reminders of life at the former airfield.

The airfield of Kenley has survived and is now home to the Surrey Hill Gliding Club and No. 615 Volunteer Gliding School.

Returning to St Luke's Church on Whyteleafe Hill it is worth taking a few minutes to visit the churchyard. Part of it has the graves of those killed whilst serving at Kenley during the Second World War with the words 'To the perpetual memory of all those who served at Royal Air Force Kenley'. Amongst the graves is that of Sergeant Peter Walley, who was killed on 18 August whilst serving with No. 615 Squadron. He was just twenty years old and, most appropriately, is buried alongside five of the ground crew who were killed during the same attack that No. 615 Squadron was trying to prevent.

Squadron	From	To	Aircraft	Sqn Code
64 Sqn	Start (16/5/40)	18/8/40	Spitfire	SH
615 Sqn	Start (20/5/40)	28/8/40	Hurricane	KW
616 Sqn	19/8/40	2/9/40	Spitfire	QJ
253 Sqn	29/8/40	End (2/1/41)	Hurricane	SW
66 Sqn	3/9/40	10/9/40	Spitfire	RB
501 Sqn	10/9/40	End (16/12/40)	Hurricane	SD

Summary of Squadrons at Kenley

Part of the churchyard at St Luke's in Whyteleafe is 'To the perpetual memory of all those who served at RAF Kenley'. One of the graves is that of twenty-year old Sergeant Peter Walley of No. 615 Sqn, who was killed defending the airfield on 18 August. Buried alongside him are five of the station personnel killed during the same attack.

Croydon

Located to the south-west of the town of Croydon in Surrey, the origins of this famous airfield date back to 1915. With the increasing number of Zeppelin air raids, it was necessary to boost the home defences around London and one site considered suitable for the Royal Flying Corps was New Barn Farm at the village of Beddington. The airfield at first took the name of the village and was developed with limited facilities. Beddington Aerodrome was home to a detachment of No. 39 (Home Defence) Squadron from early 1916 to cover the approaches to London from the south-east, but was also used as a training facility for the remainder of the First World War. A second airfield within a mile of Beddington, called Waddon Aerodrome, was developed as an aircraft factory and opened in early 1918. Whilst it was not a fully developed airfield, the land around the factory was used for test-flying aircraft.

After the First World War Beddington was initially used to receive aircraft returning from France but the newly formed RAF had no use for the airfield in the post-war era. The RAF left Beddington early in 1920 and the airfield became home to civilian flying. At about the same time, Waddon was sold to Handley Page. At that period after the war there were few developed airfields as close to London in the south-east. The close proximity of the two sites of Beddington and Waddon, and the vision of investors and developers at the time, lead to them being combined and the site became known as Croydon Aerodrome.

The expansion of Croydon was rapid. Flights were soon available to Paris and Zurich and Croydon was often referred to as 'the Continental Airport' or 'London Terminal'. In 1924 all the British commercial airlines merged to become Imperial Airways and further European routes followed. By 1927, Croydon had become the world's first international airport, with destinations including Cairo and Delhi. The airfield was also involved in various historic events during the period. Alan Cobham flew from Croydon to Capetown and back in 1925–6. Charles Lindbergh flew into Croydon in 1927 at the end of his historic first solo flight across the Atlantic in the *Spirit of St Louis*; there was an estimated crowd of 120,000 there to meet him. Bert Hinkler made the first flight to Australia (Croydon to Darwin) in 1928 and this record was broken by Charles Kingsford-Smith in the following year. In 1930, Amy Johnson left Croydon to become the first woman to fly solo from the UK to Australia.

Unsurprisingly, the interest shown in Croydon by the German airline Lufthansa increased throughout the 1930s. More crews flew

One of Croydon's new hangars built just before the Second World War shown here in camouflage, probably during the early months of the war.

into England and routes often passed over Fighter Command stations as Germany continued to build up its intelligence of the airfields and the navigation features approaching London. The last Lufthansa flight left Croydon just a matter of days before the outbreak of the Second World War.

Imperial Airways dispersed its fleet as Croydon was prepared for military operations. When the Second World War began Hurricanes of Nos 3 and 17 Squadrons and Gladiators of No. 615 Squadron arrived at Croydon but none of the units stayed and there were several changes of squadron and personnel during the opening months of the war.

In July 1940 Croydon was home to Hurricanes of No. 111 Squadron and No. 1 (RCAF) Squadron. Both units had only recently moved there but there was a significant difference in the levels of experience of the squadrons. No. 111 was fully operational and had already seen action over France, whereas the Canadians were non-operational, having only just arrived in England.

The pilots of No. 111 Squadron were in action on the opening day of the Battle of Britain when they encountered Do17s of KG2 and Bf109s of JG51 off Folkestone in the early afternoon. It was during this action that a Bf109 shot down Flying Officer Tom Higgs, who then collided with a Do17 at about 6,000 ft. Although he managed to bale out, his body was later washed ashore and he has since been officially recognized as Fighter Command's first casualty of the Battle of Britain due to enemy action.

On 11 August five of No. 111 Squadron's Hurricanes failed to return to Croydon following action with Bf109s and Do17s off Margate; four pilots were killed during what was a disastrous day for the airfield. Although the Squadron had been constantly in action since the opening day of the battle, the first weeks were relatively quiet for those on the ground. That all changed in the late afternoon of 15 August when fifteen Bf110s of *Erprobungsgruppe* 210, escorted by Bf109s, bombed the airfield. The attack took place at 6.30 p.m. and lasted no more than ten minutes, but nevertheless caused significant damage. Apart from the obvious craters across the airfield, the hangars had been hit, causing considerable damage and the armoury and the officers' mess had both been destroyed. Six airmen were killed during the attack. The damage and casualties might have been greater had the attackers not been disrupted by the Hurricanes of No. 111 Squadron in the defence of their own airfield. Some bombs missed the airfield and caused heavy civilian casualties in the local vicinity. More than sixty civilians were killed and nearly 200 injured. It was a bad day for the local community.

Erprobungsgruppe 210 paid a high price for its mistake in attacking Croydon – it is believed the target should have been Kenley. Six Bf110s and one Bf109 were shot down with six of the aircrew killed and the other seven captured. The most significant loss was the loss of the *Gruppe Kommandeur*, *Hauptman* Walter Rubensdörffer, who was shot down by fighters on his way home. His aircraft crashed at Rotherfield in East Sussex; both he and his crewman were killed. Two of the other Bf110s were shot down by pilots of No. 111 Squadron. Sergeant Bill Dymond was credited with one that crashed to the east of Reigate and Flight Lieutenant Stan Connors and Sergeant Tom Wallace shared the destruction of a Bf110 that crashed at Horley in Surrey. The three other Bf110s were all shot down by RAF fighters as they tried desperately to make their escape. One crashed at Ightham in Kent, one crashed at Hawkhurst in Kent, and one force landed at Hooe in Sussex. The Bf109 came down just south of Tunbridge Wells.

The damage caused to Croydon meant it was a couple of days before the airfield became fully operational again and No. 111 Squadron operated temporarily from Hawkinge. Just three days later, on 18 August, there was a further attack on Croydon by Do17s from medium level. Fortunately there were no casualties but there was more damage to the airfield, in particular to one of the hangars. Apart from a number of large craters around the airfield, however, there was no further significant damage. Some bombs also fell in the vicinity of the airfield during the early hours of 26 August.

No. 111 Squadron was down to just nine pilots. It left Croydon on 19 August, changing places with No. 85 Squadron at Debden. The recent attacks led to a change of plan; the Hurricanes of No. 85 Squadron were now more dispersed with the squadron occupying the western area of the airfield close to Plough Lane North. No. 85 Squadron remained at Croydon for just two weeks before moving north for a rest. It had earlier been in France and its move to Croydon during August proved costly. On the 29th the squadron lost three Hurricanes with one pilot, the Canadian Flight Lieutenant Harry Hamilton, killed. He was attacked by Bf109s over Winchelsea and crashed near the ruins of Camber Castle; he is buried in Folkestone New Cemetery in Kent.

Croydon was attacked again during the afternoon of 31 August, this time by Do17s at low level. No. 85 Squadron had just got airborne ahead of the attackers and managed to intercept the escorting fighters over Tunbridge Wells. Although the squadron lost two Hurricanes during the action, it did manage to destroy two Bf109s and a Bf110. Fortunately both of the hurricane pilots survived. One was Squadron Leader Peter Townsend, who baled out wounded in the foot, having destroyed one Bf109. It was his eighth kill and his third whilst operating from Croydon.

On 1 September the squadron lost four more aircraft. One of the pilots, Pilot Officer Patrick Woods-Scawen, had been with the squadron since before the war and had served in France, for which he was awarded the DFC. He was shot down over Kenley but managed to bale out. Unfortunately, his parachute failed and he was found dead five days later in the grounds of The Ivies in Kenley Lane. Tragically, as previously mentioned, Patrick's younger brother, Tony, died in similar circumstances almost exactly twenty-four hours later. Another loss for No. 85 Squadron during the engagement was Sergeant Glen Booth, who managed to bale out despite being badly burned. He was admitted to Purley Hospital but died later from his injuries. The third squadron pilot shot down was Flying Officer Arthur Gowers. He was badly burned and wounded during the action but made a good recovery, although he was later killed whilst commanding No. 183 Squadron in 1943. The fourth pilot lost was Sergeant John Ellis who had joined the squadron in May. He failed to return from the action and was posted as missing. He was just twenty-one years old and is commemorated on the Runnymede Memorial.

There were, however, successes for the squadron during its two weeks at Croydon. One of the most successful pilots was Pilot Officer 'Sammy' Allard, who had already enjoyed considerable success as a sergeant pilot during the Battle of France. During his two weeks at Croydon, Allard destroyed a Bf109 near Ramsgate on 24 August, two more off Folkestone on the 28th, two He111s over Bethenden on the 30th, a Bf109 off Dover on the 31st, and a Bf109 and a Do17 over the Channel on 1 September. This brought his personal total to nineteen enemy aircraft destroyed, which earned him a bar to his DFM and a DFC. However, the losses during the week were too much and No. 85 Squadron left Croydon on 2 September. Eighteen pilots had flown into

Croydon less than two weeks before; fourteen had been shot down, three of whom had been killed and five more badly burned or wounded.

No. 111 Squadron returned to Croydon on 3 September and joined the Spitfires of No. 72

Spitfires shown at Croydon during 1940.

Squadron, which had arrived at Croydon only the previous day, although neither squadron remained at Croydon for long. No. 111 left on 7 September and No. 72 the following week. In the six days that No. 111 was back it lost three Hurricanes and a further eight were damaged in combat. It was replaced by Hurricanes of No. 605 Squadron, which was soon in action but lost three Hurricanes in the first forty-eight hours of operations. One was shot down by Bf109s over Tunbridge Wells on 8 September and two were shot down during the late afternoon of 9 September whilst attacking He111s of KG53 over Farnborough.

Some more bombs fell in the vicinity of Croydon during the night of 11/12 September, although there were no casualties or any notable damage. No. 605 Squadron was involved in the heavy aerial fighting of 15 September. One of the squadron's successful pilots on that day was one of the flight commanders, Flight Lieutenant Archie McKellar, who destroyed two Bf109s just to the south-east of Croydon airfield and a Do17 in the Maidstone area. This brought McKellar's total to eight destroyed, including an He111 on 28 October 1939, which crashed in Scotland and was the first enemy aircraft to fall on British soil. Archie McKellar was undoubtedly one of the finest to have flown from Croydon during the Battle of Britain. He was given command of No. 605 Squadron on 29 September and whilst flying from Croydon during the battle destroyed fourteen enemy aircraft in just seven weeks. These included five Bf109s during one day on 7 October. He was decorated for gallantry three times having been awarded the DFC, a bar to the DFC and a DSO in the space of just a few weeks. Tragically, on the day after the battle was officially over, he was killed. He had been in combat with Bf109s over the Maidstone area on 1 November when he crashed near Addisham in Kent whilst trying to find a spot to make an emergency landing.

From mid-September, No. 605 Squadron operated alone from Croydon until the end of the Battle of Britain. Whilst there had been no major attacks against the airfield since the *Luftwaffe* turned on

London, it did receive several 'opportunity' attacks during late September and October. This was probably due to its close proximity to London, which would have made it an ideal target for bombers either having to ditch bombs or otherwise being unable to bomb their primary target.

No. 605 Squadron suffered four more losses during October. The first was over Westerham on the 7th when Bf109s shot down Pilot Officer Charles English. His aircraft crashed at Brasted. The second was Sergeant Peter McIntosh who was killed on the 12th when he was shot down by Bf109s off Dungeness. His aircraft crashed at Littlestone Golf Club and he is buried in St.John's churchyard, Shirley, in Croydon. The third was Flying Officer Ralph Hope who was killed on the 14th when he strayed into local defences and crashed in Tennison Road, South Norwood, on the northern side of Croydon. He was related on his mother's side to Neville Chamberlain. The following day, the 15th, the squadron's final casualty of the battle, Flight Lieutenant Ian Muirhead, was shot down by Bf109s over Maidstone. He had been the first of the squadron's pilots to be decorated when he was awarded the DFC in June for operations in France.

No. 605 Squadron's association with Croydon ended in February 1941 when it moved to Martlesham Heath. The change to offensive operations across the Channel and northern France meant that the airfields closer to the south coast were of more use operationally. Croydon therefore became a resting place and accommodated various squadrons taking a break from front-line operations. After D-Day, the facilities from its pre-war days as an airport made Croydon ideal for use by Transport Command.

With the Second World War over, a number of small commercial operators started using Croydon once more. By 1946 the military had ceased operating and it reverted to civilian and commercial flying. However, its life as an international airport was soon to come to an end. The world of aviation had moved on rapidly and the aircraft were larger. The runways at Croydon were too short for them and there was no room in the local area for extensions. British European Airways elected to operate from nearby Gatwick, which left just minor commercial companies operating from Croydon. Finally, a Government report during the mid-1950s ended Croydon's days as an airport.

During the 1960s, the western side of the site was developed for housing and other local facilities as the Roundshaw Estate and the eastern side became an industrial estate. During the 1990s the former airport terminal was refurbished as office accommodation and called Airport House.

The site can be found by taking the A23 Purley Way from the A232 at Croydon town centre towards Brighton. The site of the former airfield is almost immediately on the right-hand side (or western side) of the A23 and Airport House is about half a mile on the right, just after a major set of traffic lights. Turning right at the traffic lights gives access to the industrial estate, which now includes related road names such as Imperial Way. There is also the Aerodrome Hotel, which includes the Amy Johnson Restaurant. Access to Airport House is from the A23 by turning right immediately after the traffic lights into the main car park. There is a de Havilland Heron airliner mounted outside the building and there is additional parking at the rear.

At the rear of Airport House is the old air traffic control tower, which now accommodates the Croydon Airport Visitor Centre. It is open on the first Sunday of every month (11.00 a.m. to 4.00 p.m.) and covers the history of this famous airfield. Special visits can be arranged at other times for ten or more visitors from schools, societies

The former Air Traffic Control Tower now accommodates the Croydon Airport Visitors' Centre.

Airport House, the former passenger terminal at Croydon.

and other organizations, although a small charge may be made. Entrance is through the base of the tower and is free but donations are most welcome. Suggested donations are: £2 for adults, £1 for children and concessions, £3 for a family. The facilities include free car parking, a lift to the first floor and a souvenir stall, and there is plenty of interest for all ages. The Centre is staffed by volunteers from the Croydon Airport Society, which has over 700 members to keep alive the memory of this famous airfield. The address is: The Secretary, Croydon Airport Society, 68 Colston Road, Carshalton, Surrey, SM5 2NU. Telephone: 0208 669 1196 or 07949 536653.

Continuing along the A23 towards Brighton, for about half a mile, there is a memorial on the right side of the road, opposite playing fields, on the edge of the grassland area of the former airfield. It was provided by private funding and was unveiled on 27 October 1991 as 'a tribute to all connected with Croydon and its aerodrome who gave their lives in the air or on the ground during the Second World War'.

Next to the A23 Purley Way is a memorial which is a tribute to those who gave their lives whilst serving at Croydon during the Second World War. The memorial is on grassland, which marks the edge of the former airfield.

Squadron	From	To	Aircraft	Sqn Code
111 Sqn	Start (4/6/40)	18/8/40	Hurricane	TM
1 Sqn (RCAF)	Start (3/7/40)	15 Aug 40	Hurricane	YO
85 Sqn	19/8/40	2/9/40	Hurricane	VY
111 Sqn	3/9/40	7/9/40	Hurricane	TM
72 Sqn	1/9/40	13/9/40	Spitfire	SD
605 Sqn	7/9/40	End (25/2/41)	Hurricane	UP

Summary of Squadrons at Croydon

Redhill

Three miles to the east of Reigate in Surrey is the former airfield of Redhill, which was used during the Battle of Britain as an emergency satellite airfield for Kenley. It was developed in 1934 to accommodate the Redhill Flying Club. The RAF first used it in 1937 as a flying training school. It became a satellite airfield for Kenley just after the outbreak of the Second World War. For the first two months of the Battle of Britain there was no resident squadron and Redhill was only used for emergencies. During the latter period of the battle it was home to two squadrons, but only one was resident at any one time. The first squadron to be based there during the battle was No. 600 Squadron, which was equipped with Blenheims. The squadron moved in from Hornchurch on 12 September and operated from Redhill for one month in a night-fighter role before it moved north. Its period of night operations proved frustrating, as there was little or no success. It was early days for the radar in the Blenheim, which did not prove sufficiently reliable. The squadron moved to Catterick in Yorkshire and was replaced by No. 219 Squadron, which was also equipped with Blenheims although it had also started to receive Beaufighters. This squadron operated from Redhill, also in a night-fighter role, without any success for the rest of the battle.

After the battle the airfield was further developed and numerous fighter squadrons operated there until 1944, after which various support units moved in. After the Second World War, it was used as a reserve flying school and for civilian aviation until 1954, when flying was suspended for economic reasons. It resumed again in 1959 and Bristows Helicopters moved in during the following year. It was used by Bristows for training its pilots and engineers until 1998, although its head office remained at the airfield until 2004. The company plans to vacate the premises soon.

Redhill Aerodrome today.

Proposals to develop the site for larger commercial air travel, which included building a new terminal to handle 15 million passengers a year, seem to have come to nothing. The airfield is now operated by Redhill Aerodrome Limited and is used by civilian aircraft and helicopters. It is to the south-east of the town of Redhill, to the south of the A25 Redhill to Oxted road and to the east of the A23 Redhill to Horley road. It is not obvious from the main roads but is near the village of South Nutfield, not far from Bletchingley on the A25. The aerodrome is signposted from the A25 and A23 and is close to the main hospital. The address is: Redhill Aerodrome Limited, Terminal Building, Redhill Aerodrome, Surrey, RH1 5YP.

Squadron	From	To	Aircraft	Sqn Code
600 Sqn	12/9/40	12/10/40	Blenheim	BQ
219 Sqn	12/10/40	End (10/12/40)	Blenheim	FK

Summary of Squadrons at Redhill

Gatwick

As an international airport, London Gatwick hardly needs an introduction. Located just to the north of Crawley in West Sussex, it was first used as an airfield in 1930. By 1936 it was an airport but was increasingly used by the RAF during the build-up to the Second World War. During the Battle of Britain it was used as an emergency satellite airfield for Kenley, but it was also used by Lysanders of No. 26 Squadron, which moved in on 3 September and remained there until the following summer. On 18 September the squadron was joined by Defiants of No. 141 Squadron, which arrived from Biggin Hill to operate in a night-fighter role. They remained for a month before moving north just before the end of the battle.

Gatwick was used throughout the rest of the Second World War, after which RAF activity reduced and the station closed in 1946. In the 1950s it was chosen to be developed as London's second international airport and was reopened in 1958. The airport is a vast site and it can easily be found just to the west of Junction 9A of the M23.

Squadron	From	To	Aircraft	Sqn Code
26 Sqn	3/9/40	End (14/7/41)	Lysander	RM
141 Sqn	18/9/40	22/10/40	Defiant	TW

Summary of Squadrons at Gatwick

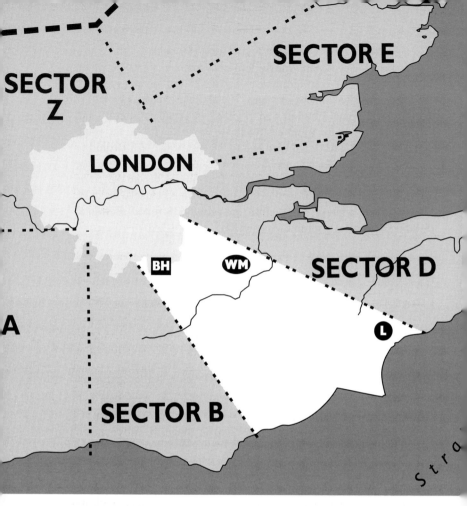

SECTOR C – AUGUST 1940

KEY:-

BH = Biggin Hill, Sector Airfield

WM = West Malling, Forward Operating Airfield

L = Lympne, Forward Operating Airfield

CHAPTER FIVE

BIGGIN HILL SECTOR
SECTOR C

The Biggin Hill Sector, or Sector C, ran from the Kenley Sector in the west, between Eastbourne and Hastings on the coast north-west to Croydon, then along the south-east of London almost to the Thames and south-east to a point just west of Dover. From many of the *Luftwaffe* bases in northern France, the shortest distance to London took the German bombers directly through this sector and, unsurprisingly, this airspace was often the busiest during the Battle of Britain.

There were just two airfields of No. 11 Group within the sector. The sector airfield of Biggin Hill itself and West Malling, which was also used as a satellite for Kenley as well as a forward operating airfield for Biggin Hill. The group also used Lympne as a forward operating airfield during the Battle of Britain and brief details of this site are also included. However, the continuous attacks meant that Lympne was unable to take any real part in the Battle of Britain other than as a valuable emergency landing ground for RAF fighters. Other targets of interest to the *Luftwaffe* within the sector included the radar sites at Rye and Fairlight near Hastings.

Biggin Hill

Located about 6 miles to the south-east of Croydon, Biggin Hill first opened in February 1917. Its first resident unit was No. 141 Squadron, which arrived in February 1918 as a home defence squadron for the protection of London. With the war over the squadron moved out in March 1919 and disbanded soon after. Unlike many other airfields, which had no post-war military future, Biggin Hill remained a front-line station for the RAF. In May 1923 Snipes of No. 56 Squadron moved in from Hawkinge. Soon after, the squadron re-equipped with Grebes, and later Siskins, before it left Biggin Hill in October 1927. Following its departure major development began, with the construction of new hangars, technical and administration buildings, and domestic accommodation. Work was completed in 1932 and No. 23 Squadron, with Harts, and No. 32 Squadron, with Bulldogs moved in from Kenley. Both squadrons served together at Biggin until No. 23

Squadron moved out at the end of 1936. No. 32 remained at Biggin until the outbreak of the Second World War.

During the early days of the Second World War Biggin Hill was home to Nos 32 and 79 Squadrons, both equipped with the new Hawker Hurricane, and No. 601 Squadron equipped with Blenheims. When the Germans invaded France and the Low Countries, No. 79 Squadron moved to France. No. 32 moved around in support of operations across the Channel but returned to Biggin in June. By that time there had been further construction work at the airfield, which included the hardening of the main runway (1,600 yards).

When the Battle of Britain began Biggin Hill was one of Fighter Command's most vital airfields and was home to Hurricanes of No. 32 Squadron and Spitfires of No. 610 Squadron. Together with Kenley, it covered the approaches to London from the south and south-east.

The Spitfires were in action on the opening day of the battle with Bf109s over Dover during the late morning. The first pilot lost due to enemy action was Pilot Officer Peter Litchfield of No. 610 Squadron, who was shot down over the Channel by a Bf109 of JG51 during the morning of 18 July. Two days later No. 32 Squadron lost its first pilot when a Bf109 of JG51 shot down Sub-Lieutenant Geoffrey Bulmer off Dover. Neither pilot was found; Peter Litchfield is remembered on the Runnymede Memorial and Geoffrey Bulmer on the Fleet Air Arm Memorial at Lee-on-Solent.

A further loss during July was Squadron Leader Andrew Smith, who had been commanding officer of No. 610 Squadron since the end of May. He was killed when his Spitfire crashed whilst attempting to land at Hawkinge following combat with Bf109s over the Channel during the afternoon of 25 July. Command of the squadron was given to Squadron Leader John Ellis, who had been a flight commander with the squadron since the outbreak of war. By the time he took command he had been awarded the DFC for seven confirmed kills and was one of the RAF's first aces of the battle. He achieved five of his kills during July whilst operating from Biggin Hill, including three Bf109s on the day he took command of the squadron. He commanded No. 610 Squadron for the rest of the battle and destroyed ten aircraft during his time at Biggin Hill.

On 11 August No. 610 Squadron lost two Spitfires when they failed to return following combat with Bf109s over the Channel; both pilots were killed. On 15 August No. 32 Squadron lost Pilot Officer Douglas Grice when he was shot down in flames. He managed to bale out and landed in the sea. He was rescued and admitted to hospital but was to

Spitfires of No. 610 Sqn, which served at Biggin Hill from the opening day of the battle until it moved north on 12 September for a rest.

take no further part in flying operations during the war. It was a sad loss to the squadron as he was one of its most experienced pilots, having been with it since 1938, and had brought his total to five enemy aircraft destroyed before he was shot down. The following day No. 610 Squadron also lost one of its more experienced pilots when one of its flight commanders, Flight Lieutenant William Warner, failed to return following combat with Bf109s off Dungeness. He had been with the squadron since 1937 and was just twenty-one years old.

The amount of air activity at Biggin Hill during the month peaked on 12 and 15 August when the three squadrons flew more than 100 sorties between them on both days. The first attack against the airfield took place at about 1.30 p.m. on 18 August and lasted more than an hour, leaving it cratered, with damage to the main runway. Fortunately, most of the bombs fell on the golf course nearby. The station commander, Group Captain Richard Grice, had taken the initiative to order both squadrons into the air, which almost certainly prevented any losses of fighters on the ground. However, No. 32 Squadron was at an extreme disadvantage as its Hurricanes struggled to gain height. Two were shot down within minutes and two had to make forced landings. Fortunately, all four pilots were safe, although two baled out wounded. One of the wounded was Flight Lieutenant Humphrey Russell, one of the flight commanders, who had joined the squadron in 1936. His

77

Hurricane crashed at Edenbridge and Russell was admitted to hospital but returned in April 1941 to command the squadron. Another pilot to have a lucky escape was Flying Officer Alan 'Shag' Eckford, who managed to force land his Hurricane back at Biggin Hill. He had scored his first victory in France during May and had brought his total to four kills when he destroyed a Bf109 north of Canterbury during the action of 18 August. Also shot down during the same action was the commanding officer, Squadron Leader Michael Crossley, who baled out unhurt. He had destroyed seven enemy aircraft during the Battle of France and was awarded the DFC. During his time at Biggin Hill he destroyed a further thirteen aircraft, twelve of them in a period of just two weeks during August. This brought his total to twenty enemy aircraft destroyed, for which he was awarded the DSO. He remained in command of the squadron until the end of the battle.

The attack on Biggin Hill on 18 August was the first of many. During the following two weeks there were almost daily attacks as the airfield became a major target for the *Luftwaffe*. No. 79 Squadron replaced No. 32 Squadron on 27 August and three days later the airfield was left in near ruin as it suffered further attacks. The first was at midday from medium level and the second, at about 6.00 p.m., was from low level. It was the latter, by Ju88s, which caused the most damage. There was little time for the station's personnel to take cover as there had been just a few minutes' warning. The attack proved to be devastating. A hangar, several technical buildings, workshops and barrack blocks were destroyed, and several more buildings damaged. Furthermore, most of the station's transport was destroyed or damaged and all the gas and electrical supplies were cut. Thirty-nine personnel were killed and more than twenty wounded.

After the raiders had gone, the station was silent and the scene was one of complete devastation. Some personnel taking cover in a trench near the guardroom had a lucky escape, having been almost buried alive when the trench caved in following an almost direct hit. Others had elected not to take cover in the airfield's shelters but to take their chances out in the open; there were several casualties after one shelter was destroyed by a direct hit. The airfield had lost its communications, which meant that it was unable to carry out its role as a sector airfield and control was temporarily passed to Hornchurch. This extended Hornchurch's area of responsibility from the Thames Estuary south-eastwards to the coast and its operations room temporarily controlled five airfields (Hornchurch, Rochford, Biggin Hill, Gravesend and Redhill) and six squadrons.

Known locally as 'The Leaves Green Dornier', this Do17 of KG76 came down in a farmer's field next to Biggin Hill on 18 August 1940. The aircraft had been hit by the airfield's defences during its attack against Kenley and was then finished off by Hurricanes of No. 111 Sqn.

The same position today. When visiting the site it can be seen that *Hauptmann* Roth and his crew were just a matter of 100 yards short of making an emergency landing at Biggin. Nevertheless, the crew survived and were taken prisoners.

The temporary loss of Biggin Hill was a significant blow to No. 11 Group. It was, indeed, pivotal to the success of Fighter Command and every effort was made to restore its communications. However, there was little water and accommodation had to be found in the local area as so much had been destroyed during the attack. Darkness soon came, which prevented much work being done until first light. Repair work was also hampered the following morning by continual warnings of further attacks. Indeed there were two more attacks during the afternoon, the first at 1.00 p.m. and the second at 5.30 p.m., which caused more serious damage. The operations building suffered significant damage, which meant that the operations room had to be moved away from the airfield. It made its temporary home at a local shop but was later moved to an old Victorian house called Towerfields, 2 miles to the north of the airfield. By the end of the day, Biggin Hill had re-established some communications with the squadron's dispersal and with HQ No. 11 Group.

On 31 August No. 72 Squadron operated from Biggin Hill for the day, losing one pilot in combat during the early evening over Dungeness. Flying Officer Edgar Wilcox is buried in All Saints churchyard at Staplehurst.

The following day Biggin Hill was once again a major target. The attack occurred at about 1.30 p.m. from medium level and, again, the communications buildings came off worst. The airfield had now suffered five concentrated air attacks in forty-eight hours. The damage caused was significant

Pilot Officer Geoffrey Roscoe had only just completed his flying training when he was sent to No. 79 Squadron at Biggin Hill in early September 1940. Although he survived the battle he was killed in February 1942 whilst serving with No. 87 Squadron.

and the ground crew continued to work tirelessly to keep the airfield open. There was a further attack on 6 September but no further significant damage was caused. The station had come desperately close to ceasing to function as an airfield. There was hardly a building intact and all services were cut off. As a result, several sections were moved out to nearby Keston. However, the airfield survived, although the combined effect of this period of sustained air attacks meant that just one squadron could operate from the airfield at a time: No. 92 Squadron moved in on 8 September and No. 610 Squadron went north for a rest.

Biggin Hill had been one of the two most bombed airfields in Fighter Command; the other was Hornchurch. Fortunately, the *Luftwaffe* turned its attention to London on 7 September, which gave the pilots and ground crew a rest from the continuous barrage of the past week and meant that the airfield facilities could be repaired.

When it was back to some sort of normality, Defiants of No. 141 Squadron moved in on 13 September but they remained for just a few days and then No. 72 Squadron returned.

On 27 September, two Spitfires of No. 72 Squadron were shot down over Sevenoaks with both pilots killed. No. 92 Squadron lost three Spitfires with all three pilots lost. Both squadrons suffered further casualties during early October, including the loss of two Spitfires of No. 92 Squadron on 10 October when they collided during an attack on a Do17 over Tangmere. Pilot Officer Desmond Williams and Flying Officer John Drummond were both already aces at the ages of twenty and twenty-one respectively, with Drummond having scored four of his victories during his short time at Biggin Hill; both pilots were killed.

No. 74 Squadron arrived at Biggin Hill on 15 October to replace No. 72. In command was the experienced South African ace, Squadron Leader 'Sailor' Malan. By the time he arrived at Biggin Hill, Malan had already been credited with at least ten enemy aircraft destroyed and had been awarded the DFC and bar. He added five more Bf109s to his total whilst at Biggin Hill and went on to be credited with twenty-seven kills for which he was also awarded the DSO and bar before the end of the war.

Another of the great aces of the war to make his name whilst operating from Biggin during the latter weeks of the battle was Sergeant Donald Kingaby, who scored the first three of his twenty-one kills whilst serving as a sergeant pilot with No. 92 Squadron. Although he had previously claimed a number of aircraft as damaged, Kingaby was credited with his first kill, a Bf109 near Rochester, on 12 October. He destroyed another Bf109 over the Channel on 15 October and a Do17 east of Deal on 24 October. Although the battle was officially over, Kingaby added five more Bf109s to his total before he left Biggin Hill in January 1941 and was awarded the first of his three DFMs – the only time a DFM and two bars was ever awarded.

No. 74 Squadron had been amongst the first squadrons to receive the Spitfire II and it operated this type from Biggin Hill during the final days of the Battle of Britain. Although the battle was in its final two weeks, the new arrivals still suffered the loss of four pilots, including the last Biggin Hill pilot to die during the battle, Sergeant John Scott, who was shot down on 27 October over Maidstone; his Spitfire crashed at Elmsted Court.

Fighter Command turned to offensive operations during 1941 and several fighter squadrons operated from Biggin Hill during the next couple of years; all were equipped with more powerful and better-armed Spitfires. The Spitfires were joined by Typhoons during late 1942. Biggin Hill also became home to three Canadian squadrons during 1943 and they remained until April 1944.

The V-1 attacks against London brought flying to an end at Biggin Hill as it was in the line of fire for London. The airfield was temporarily transferred to Balloon Command during the phase of the V-1 attacks but returned to flying duties in October. Towards the end of the war Biggin Hill was used by fighter squadrons escorting Bomber Command in daylight raids over Europe. By the end, transport aircraft had increasingly used the airfield and it was officially transferred to Transport Command. However, over the next year transport flights reduced and it was transferred to Reserve Command in August 1946. It was given a new lease of life in 1949 when it was transferred back to Fighter Command. Throughout the 1950s it was home to RAF jet fighters but the close proximity to London and the increasingly crowded airspace meant that the RAF ceased flying operations in 1958.

Biggin Hill was then divided into two. The RAF retained the north side, known as North Camp, to accommodate the Officers' Selection Centre, which opened in 1959, and later the Aircrew Selection Centre, which opened in 1962. The southern half, South Camp, was leased to Surrey Aviation for private flying and, when Croydon Airport closed in 1959, many of its operators moved to Biggin Hill.

Bromley Council took over the airfield in 1973, which left North Camp with just the buildings used by the RAF for selection. In 1979 the Government decided to close it down with the exception of the officers' mess and St George's Chapel. The RAF finally moved out in 1992, when officer and aircrew selection moved to Cranwell, and the airfield has since been renamed London Biggin Hill Airport.

The airfield is very easy to find. It is well signposted from the M25 (Junction 4) and is found by following the A21 towards Bromley and then taking the A232 and A233. Having turned left towards Westerham, at the crossroads known as 'Keston Mark', the road passes Towerfields about 400 yards on the right side. The old Victorian mansion which was used as the temporary sector operations room following attacks on Biggin Hill during August 1940, has now been developed into flats. The original tower on the mansion has been demolished but the building has remained as a lasting monument.

Continuing south towards Westerham for just over a mile, the first part of the airfield reached is the entrance to Biggin Hill Airport on the left. The airport has been upgraded for the operation of small commercial airliners and business jets, which has also included the introduction of handling facilities and the construction of a passenger terminal and a new hangar. However, a barrier prevents those without permission proceeding further and there is little to see at that point. Continuing towards Westerham, the road passes through the original part of RAF Biggin Hill. St. George's Chapel of Remembrance can be seen on the left side and access is through a gate at the front of the Chapel, which passes between the replicas of a Spitfire and Hurricane. The original station church was destroyed by fire in 1946 but the Chaplain at the time, the Reverend King, had the idea of building a permanent memorial chapel to commemorate the allied aircrew who gave their lives whilst operating from Biggin Hill during the Second

Towerfields near Keston Mark has now been converted to flats but was once the temporary Operations Room for Biggin Hill following attacks against the airfield in August 1940.

World War. After donations and a grant from the Air Ministry, building of the chapel began and Air Chief Marshal Lord Dowding laid the foundation stone. The Bishop of Rochester dedicated St George's Chapel of Remembrance on 10 November 1951. The design has retained the internal plain brick appearance of the original station church, which meant so much to those who had served and worshipped at Biggin Hill.

The chapel is ornately furnished and there are twelve beautiful stained-glass windows, which have been donated by various individuals and organizations. Each is to a common theme, the Cloud of Witnesses, and depicts the spirit of a pilot holding a squadron badge of one of the seven squadrons that actually served at Biggin Hill or of Fighter Command or one of its groups. In addition to the general theme, the windows contain some interesting detail. Those at the west end immortalize the Spitfire and Hurricane, and the second window from the back on the northern side has a mosquito insect painted in the lower right-hand corner; this is because the glazier flew Mosquitos during the Second World War. One of the windows was given by an anonymous donor and bears the inscription, 'And some there be who have no memorial.' The west window in the St George's Room was installed as part of the fortieth anniversary of the Battle of Britain and the remaining four windows in the room were installed in 1985 to commemorate the part played by the ground branches of the RAF. Of particular interest is the three Military Medals in the lower right-hand corner of the Ground Control window, which were awarded to three members of the WAAF following their bravery during two attacks on the airfield in the Battle of Britain. The gilded wooden eagle on the large lectern was privately donated and the small wooden lectern was donated by the Belgian Air Force. The squadron standard of No. 92

St George's Chapel of Remembrance is still used by t
community at Biggin Hill and is open daily to visito

Squadron is also displayed in the chapel and the bible on the altar is believed to have come from the original station church, having been found on the site when it was cleared in 1949.

The Memorial Chapel is still used as a church within the community and it is open daily to visitors between 10.00 a.m. to 4.00 p.m., although times may vary. There are weekly services, as well as special services of remembrance on Battle of Britain Sunday and Remembrance Day. The replica Hurricane is of L1710 'AL-D' of No. 79 Squadron, which intercepted a raid on Biggin Hill by 100 enemy aircraft on 5 September 1940. The Spitfire replica is of N3194 'GR-Z' of No. 92 Squadron. More details of the Chapel can be obtained by telephone on 01959 570353.

Continuing towards Westerham, the airfield can be clearly seen on the left. At the mini-roundabout turn left to reach the private flying clubs that continue to use the airfield; Biggin Hill is the most popular light aviation venue south of London. The flying clubs provide pleasure trips, private flying, helicopter flying and many other services.

Squadron	From	To	Aircraft	Sqn Code
32 Sqn	Start (4/6/40)	27/8/40	Hurricane	KT
610 Sqn	Start (2/7/40)	12/9/40	Spitfire	DW
79 Sqn	27/8/40	7/9/40	Hurricane	AL
72 Sqn	31/8/40	1/9/40	Spitfire	SD
	14/9/40	12/10/40		
141 Sqn	13/9/40	18/9/40	Defiant	TW
92 Sqn	8/9/40	End (9/1/41)	Spitfire	GR
74 Sqn	15/10/40	End (20/2/41)	Spitfire	ZP

Summary of Squadrons at Biggin Hill

ooking north-east across the irfield, Biggin Hill is still very ctive and is now used both as an irport and for private flying.

West Malling

Seven miles to the north-west of Maidstone in Kent is the town of West Malling. The airfield was originally known as King's Hill. Although the site was first used as a landing ground during the First World War, it was not until 1930 that it was opened as an airfield. Initially used for private flying, the airfield became Maidstone Airport in 1932 and then Malling Aero Club in 1935. Following the outbreak of the Second World War, the RAF took it over just before the Battle of Britain.

The airfield had grass runways and was used during the battle as a satellite for Kenley and a forward operating airfield for Biggin Hill. The only resident unit when the battle opened was No. 26 (Army Co-operation) Squadron, equipped with Lysanders. On 12 July No. 141 Squadron arrived from Turnhouse in Scotland and its first action took place just after midday on 19 July when the Defiants were engaged by Bf109s of JG51 over the Channel. The outcome was devastating. Six Defiants operating out of Hawkinge during the day were shot down in a matter of a few minutes and one returned to Malling badly damaged. Although they claimed four successes during the fierce battle with the Bf109s, this single action cost No. 141 Squadron dearly and effectively wiped out the squadron in one go. Six aircraft were lost and ten of the crew were either killed or missing. This disaster resulted in No. 141 Squadron being posted north just two days later, although it would later return south as a night-fighter squadron.

The departure of No. 141 Squadron left just No. 26 Squadron in residence at Malling. During August there were a number of attacks against the airfield, which resulted in it being out of action for much of the key period of the battle. One attack took place from low level without any warning at 7.30 a.m. on 10 August. Fourteen bombs landed, causing damage to two aircraft and several buildings. The attack lasted just a few minutes but a number of personnel were injured, one of whom later died. There was a further attack at 7.00 p.m. on 15 August when bombs were dropped from medium altitude killing two airmen and also causing further damage to buildings. During the following day there was another attack, which resulted in damage to a hangar. Two days later more damage was caused to the new hangars and three Lysanders were written off. Fortunately there were no casualties but this brought the total number of attacks to four in just eight days.

There were two more attacks during the last week of August and two more during the first week of September, which resulted in significant damage to the airfield and the loss of communications. The intense period of attack forced No. 26 Squadron to leave the airfield on 3 September. On the 10th a lone Do17 attacked during the late afternoon killing six soldiers. On the afternoon of 15 September an He111 of KG53 force-landed at West Malling after it had been hit by RAF fighters during an attack against London Docks. Two members of the crew were captured but the other two were killed.

During the following three days there were daily attacks against Malling and six more during the following four weeks. It was the end of October before the airfield was ready for operations once more. By then the raids had stopped and the damage had been cleared up enough to allow Spitfires of No. 66 Squadron to move in on 30 October, the penultimate day of the battle.

It was not until the spring of 1941 that West Malling was restored to full status. Several squadrons operated from the airfield during 1942 and 1943, including fighters of the US Eighth Air Force, which were involved in escorting bombers across Europe. In 1944 it became the main operating airfield for fighters trying to shoot down the German V-1 flying bombs. In the second half of that year, it closed for major development work, including the construction of a concrete runway, which took until the end of the war to complete.

The airfield reopened just as the war came to an end and was used to receive prisoners of war returning to the UK. It then became home to various types of aircraft including the RAF's new jet fighter, the Meteor, and later the Javelin. It closed as an operational airfield in 1960 and was placed on care and maintenance before the RAF moved out in 1967. The US Navy later used it for a short period before the local council bought it in 1970 and converted its buildings into office accommodation.

The site is some way out of the village and covers more than 500 acres of land. Kent County Council has developed much of it as the King's Hill council offices, and the rest has been used for businesses, housing and a golf course. However, many of the RAF buildings from the post-war period remain.

A memorial was erected and unveiled on 9 June 2002 to mark the site of the airfield and it stands as a testament to the military and civilian personnel who served there. It includes the names of some of the famous airmen who flew from West Malling during the Second World War: Wing Commander Peter Townsend, Wing Commander Bob Braham, Wing Commander John 'Cats-Eyes' Cunningham and Wing Commander Guy Gibson. Next to the memorial stands a statue of an unnamed airman with the crests of the squadrons that operated from

At the end of Gibson Drive in Kings Hill, a memorial was erected in June 2002 to mark the site of the former airfield of West Malling. Next to the memorial stands a statue of an unnamed airman.

the airfield during and after the war.

The site can be found by taking the A228 from Junction 4 of the M20. Proceed along the A228, by-passing the town of West Malling, for about 3 miles until you see the King's Hill council complex on the left. Turn left and proceed down Gibson Drive as far as possible (about a mile), across a large roundabout, to reach the memorial and statue. Also in the vicinity is the former air traffic control tower, which can be

Amongst the large redevelopment Kings Hill, the former Air Traffic Contr Tower of West Malling has survived a can be found in Queen's Stree

found by returning back down Gibson Drive, turning left at the roundabout into Forest Way and then next left into Discovery Way. Proceed down Discovery Way, across a roundabout and then turn left into Fortune Way. Take the next left into Queen's Street and the tower is immediately on the right.

Squadron	From	To	Aircraft	Sqn Code
26 Sqn	Start (8/6/40)	3/9/40	Lysander	RM
141 Sqn	12/7/40	21/7/40	Defiant	TW
66 Sqn	30/10/40	End (7/11/40)	Spitfire	RB/LZ

Summary of Squadrons at West Malling

Lympne

Lympne is about 7 miles to the west of Folkestone in Kent. The origins of the airfield date back to the First World War, when the site was developed in 1916 as an emergency landing ground for home defence units of the Royal Flying Corps. At the end of the war it was retained, and was used for civil aviation during the 1920s. The RAF maintained an interest, and auxiliary squadrons used the airfield for summer camps during the late 1920s. As the RAF increased its number of airfields during the build-up to the Second World War, it increased its use of Lympne from 1937. The airfield was transferred to Fighter Command in 1939 but initially had no resident unit. When France fell in the spring of 1940 the airfield was increasingly used by aircraft returning across the Channel.

By the time the Battle of Britain opened Lympne was a forward operating airfield for No. 11 Group. Various squadrons deployed in from their home bases and operated from the airfield during the hours of daylight before returning to their bases in the evening. The first attack on the airfield occurred on 12 August when fifteen Do17s of KG2 carried out a low-level attack, which destroyed six of the original hangars, including several private aircraft that were inside, as well as domestic accommodation; one airman was killed. A second attack took place soon after, which resulted in the airfield being temporarily out of action. A minor attack on the following day and a more devastating attack by forty Ju87s of StG1 on 15 August meant that Lympne was effectively out of action for the following few weeks.

Station personnel moved out and were accommodated in the village and local area. Port Lympne became the temporary officers' mess,

French House the sergeants' mess and Lympne Palace the airmen's feeder. The airfield was again a target on 1 September. The continuous attacks on the airfield, and its proximity to the south-east coast meant that there was little warning of an attack and it took no real further part in the Battle of Britain, other than as an emergency landing ground for RAF fighters.

It was not until the spring of 1941 that Lympne was used operationally for offensive sweeps across the Channel. The facilities were later upgraded so that up to three squadrons at a time could operate there. At the end of the Second World War the airfield was initially placed on care and maintenance, although it was then used for commercial scheduled flights across the Channel into France and Belgium. It was renamed Ashford Airport in 1968 and improved facilities were constructed. However, a decline in the need for air freight and commercial routes across the Channel resulted in its gradual demise during the 1970s. The site was gradually taken over and it is now Lympne Industrial Park. Port Lympne, which was the location of the wartime officers' mess, is now part of Port Lympne Wild Animal Park and Gardens.

The site of the former airfield can be found near Junction 11 of the M20. Take the A20 towards Ashford, past Folkestone Race Course, turn left at the B2067 (signposted towards the Wild Animal Park) and the industrial park will soon be found on the left. The industrial park and the land to the south of the B2067, about 3 miles to the west of the village of West Hythe, is the area of the former airfield, although evidence has all but disappeared.

Behind some surviving buildings, the Lympne Industrial Park now marks the site of the former airfield.

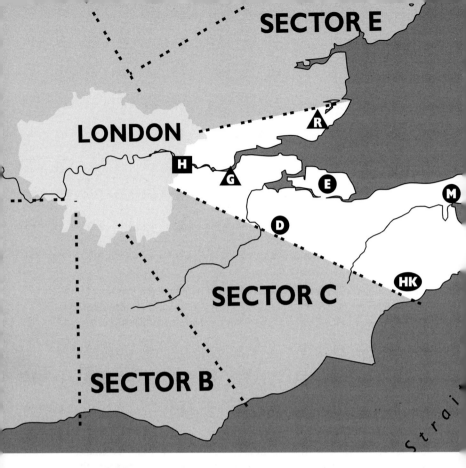

SECTOR D – AUGUST 1940

KEY:-

H = Hornchurch, Sector Airfield

R = Rochford, Satellite Airfield

G = Gravesend, Satellite Airfield

M = Manston, Forward Operating Airfield

HK = Hawkinge, Forward Operating Airfield

D = Detling, Coastal Command Airfield

E = Eastchurch, Coastal Command Airfield

CHAPTER SIX

HORNCHURCH SECTOR
SECTOR D

The far south-east of England was protected by the Hornchurch Sector, or Sector D, which included the area from the boundary with the Biggin Hill Sector and northwards to cover the Thames estuary. The shortest route across the Channel from northern France took the *Luftwaffe* across from Calais to Dover and many of the attacks on London passed through the Hornchurch Sector. Unsurprisingly, the airspace was often one of the busiest during the Battle of Britain. Geographically, there were five of No. 11 Group's airfields within this sector, the most in any one sector. Hornchurch was the sector airfield and there were two forward operating airfields at Hawkinge and Manston.

Although the two other No. 11 Group airfields were geographically located in the Hornchurch Sector, Gravesend was used as a satellite airfield for Biggin Hill and Rochford as a satellite for both Hornchurch and North Weald during the Battle of Britain. In addition to the five No. 11 Group airfields, there were two Coastal Command airfields, Detling and Eastchurch. Their prime purpose was to provide operational airfields to help protect shipping in the Channel and to locate and counter any German raids from the sea. However, the location of both airfields south-east of London meant that both were occasionally used by No. 11 Group during the Battle of Britain and brief details are included for completeness.

Apart from the airfields, other targets of interest to the *Luftwaffe* within the sector were the radar sites at Dover, Foreness and Dunkirk. There were large anti-aircraft batteries near Dover and Margate, as well as on either side of the Thames estuary covering the eastern approach to London. There was also an Observer Corps centre near Detling.

No visit to this sector would be complete without calling at the National Memorial to the Battle of Britain at Capel-le-Ferne. It is situated just to the north of Folkestone, close to the former Battle of Britain airfield at Hawkinge, and details of that are also included in this chapter.

Hornchurch

Located on the eastern side of London, this airfield was formerly known as Sutton's Farm and was first used by the Royal Flying Corps in 1915 as part of the defences of London. It was whilst operating from Sutton's Farm on the night of 2/3 September 1916 that William Leefe-Robinson of No. 39 Squadron brought down a German airship, for which he was awarded the VC. At the end of the First World War it was decided that Sutton's Farm would not be retained but the post-war RAF had a change of mind and the airfield reopened as RAF Hornchurch in 1928. It was home to various fighter squadrons during the 1930s, and when the RAF restructured in 1936 it became part of No. 11 Group, Fighter Command. As one of the RAF's principal fighter bases, much work was done during the final preparations for the Second World War and, following the German advance into France and the Low Countries, Hornchurch's squadrons were involved during the air war over France and the subsequent evacuation of Dunkirk.

When the Battle of Britain opened, Hornchurch was home to the Spitfires of Nos 65 and 74 Squadrons, and both were involved during the opening phase of the battle. In particular, No. 74 Squadron was involved in combat with Bf109s over the Channel during the opening morning followed by further action with Do17s and Bf109s above Dover during the early afternoon. One of the squadron pilots to enjoy his first success during the day was Flying Officer John Mungo-Park, who destroyed a Do17 south of Folkestone. He had joined No. 74 Squadron at the outbreak of the war and had already seen action over Dunkirk. His kill on 10 July was the first of three whilst operating from Hornchurch.

No. 54 Squadron was officially posted to Hornchurch on 24 July but it was operating between Hornchurch and Rochford during the opening weeks of the battle and it was quite familiar with Hornchurch, as it had been its base throughout most of the 1930s. However, on this occasion, it remained for just four days, as it had lost five Spitfires and three pilots killed in just two days whilst operating from the forward operating airfield at Rochford. It was posted north to recover but returned to Hornchurch to rejoin the battle soon after. It was replaced by No. 41 Squadron, which arrived at Hornchurch on 26 July.

This Squadron suffered its first loss in combat on 28 July when a Bf109 of JG26 shot down Pilot Officer James Young over the Channel. Just three days later the squadron lost two more pilots, both killed during combat with Bf109s of JG51 on the late afternoon of 31 July.

No. 65 Squadron suffered its first pilot killed on 2 August when its commanding officer, Squadron Leader Henry Sawyer, crashed whilst taking off for a night patrol. Its first losses in combat occurred on 8 August when Sergeant David Kirton and Flight Sergeant Norman Phillips were both killed during combat with Bf109s of JG26 over Manston.

Twenty-one years old Sergeant David Kirton joined No. 65 Squadron in July 1940 but was killed just three weeks later when he was shot down by Bf109s during the action over Manston on 8 August.

On the same day, command of No. 74 Squadron was given to Squadron Leader 'Sailor' Malan when Squadron Leader Francis White was posted to HQ Fighter Command. Malan was one of the most famous pilots to have flown from Hornchurch and one of the RAF's most successful pilots during the Battle of Britain. Born in South Africa, he joined the RAF in 1935 and was posted to No. 74 Squadron in December 1936. He was credited with three enemy aircraft destroyed over Dunkirk during May and awarded the DFC in June. During his time at Hornchurch, Malan brought his personal total to nine kills for which he was awarded a bar to his DFC in August. He ended the war with twenty-seven confirmed kills and had added a DSO and bar to his decorations.

Another successful pilot serving with No. 74 Squadron at

...ny of the roads on the former site of Hornchurch have been named after those ...at flew from the airfield during the Battle of Britain. One such example is a quiet ...se overlooking the Country Park, which has been named after Sergeant David ...ton. Dewey Path is named after Pilot Officer Robert Dewey of No. 603 ...uadron who was shot down and killed on 27 October.

Hornchurch during this period was Pilot Officer Harbourne Stephen, who had scored his first victory over Dunkirk during May. He was involved throughout the day on 11 August over Dover and claimed five victories, three Bf109s and two Bf110s. Although just one Bf109 was eventually confirmed, he went on to be credited with four kills during the battle, for which he was awarded the DFC.

No. 54 Squadron returned to Hornchurch to replace No. 41 Squadron on 8 August. One of its young pilots was Flying Officer Al Deere. Born in Auckland, New Zealand, Deere had arrived in the UK in 1937 and joined the RAF. He joined No. 54 Squadron at Hornchurch in August 1938 and was heavily involved in the air war over France in May, during which he was credited with the destruction of seven enemy aircraft and awarded the DFC. Whilst operating from Hornchurch on 12 August he destroyed a Bf109 and a Bf110, and by the end of the month had brought his total to fourteen destroyed. By the time he left Hornchurch in September he had been awarded a bar to his DFC. He ended the war with some twenty confirmed kills (although the exact number varies, depending on source) for which he was also awarded a DSO.

Another Hornchurch pilot to enjoy success on 12 August was Flying Officer Paddy Finucane of No. 65 Squadron. He was born in Dublin and joined the RAF in May 1938. He was posted to No. 65 Squadron in July 1940 at the age of nineteen. His success on 12 August, a Bf109 off Deal, was his first kill and he added a second Bf109 during the following day. He went on to be credited with twenty-six confirmed kills, incredibly all against fighters: twenty-two Bf109s, three Fw190s and a Bf110. Finucane was awarded a DSO plus a DFC and bar, and was appointed Wing Leader of the Hornchurch Wing in June 1942. Sadly, whilst leading the wing over France in 1942, he was killed after attempting to ditch in the Channel having been hit by ground fire.

Also serving at Hornchurch during the Battle of Britain was Warrant Officer Ernest 'Tubby' Mayne of No. 74 Squadron who, at

Born in Dublin, Flying Officer Paddy Finucane served with No. 65 Squadron at Hornchur. He scored his first victory on 12 August a went on to be credited with twenty-six confirmed victories before he was killed on 15 July 1942 whilst leading the Hornchurc Wing over France.

thirty-nine, was the oldest man to fly as a regular squadron pilot during the battle. He was a veteran of the Royal Flying Corps and flew his final operational sortie from Hornchurch on 11 August, sharing in the destruction of two Bf110s. He survived the war, after which he retired from the RAF.

The two days of 11–12 August saw a peak of activity at Hornchurch and the most number of sorties flown by its three squadrons to date, a total of 190 during the two days, half of which were flown by No. 65 Squadron.

No. 266 Squadron replaced No. 74 on 14 August and went straight into heavy fighting, destroying ten aircraft during its first week. However, it also suffered losses. It lost two Spitfires on 15 August, with both pilots killed and, in just twenty minutes on the following day, lost five more during combat with Bf109s of JG26 over Canterbury, with three more pilots killed. In the latter engagement the first killed was the commanding officer, Squadron Leader Rod Wilkinson, whose Spitfire crashed at Eastry Court. The second was Sub-Lieutenant Henry Greenshields of the Fleet Air Arm, who had joined the squadron just before the battle opened and had destroyed a Bf109 during the action of the previous day. He failed to return after chasing Bf109s across the Channel. The third pilot to lose his life was Pilot Officer Nigel Bowen. His Spitfire was shot down in flames and crashed at Adisham. He was just twenty years old.

Hornchurch was a priority target on 18 August and No. 266 Squadron again suffered when six of its Spitfires were severely damaged during a strafing attack by Bf109s in the afternoon. These further losses proved too much and the squadron was moved north for a rest. No. 74 Squadron had moved out just a few days earlier and Hornchurch then became home to the Defiants of No. 264 Squadron and the Blenheims of No. 600 Squadron; both arrived on 22 August. The Blenheims were to be involved in night-fighter operations but the Defiants had been sent as day fighters.

No. 264 Squadron operated from Hornchurch and Manston for just one week, during which it lost seven Defiants. On 24 August the squadron intercepted Ju88s over Manston soon after midday but were mauled by the escorting Bf109s of JG3. Three Defiants were shot down with the loss of all three crews. Later in the afternoon a Bf109 of JG51 shot down another Defiant over Hornchurch; the air gunner died of his wounds. Two days later the squadron was in action with Bf109s over Thanet. In the space of twenty minutes, it lost three aircraft, with another two men missing. Two days later it lost three more during another engagement with Bf109s over Thanet; five more personnel were killed. These losses were simply too much and the Defiant had proved to be totally inadequate as a day fighter. It was no match for the Bf109, whose pilots quickly recognized its weakness in the forward sector during combat. The action of 28 August proved to be the squadron's last and it was moved back to its former base at Kirton-in-Lindsey in Lincolnshire.

The Spitfires of Nos 222 and 603 Squadrons arrived at Hornchurch to replace the Defiants and the Spitfires of No. 65 Squadron. No. 603 Squadron lacked any combat experience but it was involved in heavy fighting during its first three days, resulting in the loss of seven Spitfires. Three of these losses occurred on 28 August, when the squadron engaged Bf109s above Dover, with all three pilots killed. During the following two days the squadron lost four more aircraft, although all four pilots were saved. No. 222 Squadron also suffered losses and lost six Spitfires on 30 August during two separate actions in the late afternoon and early evening; one of the pilots was killed.

Also on 30 August, extensive damage caused during air attacks against Biggin Hill meant that that station could not carry out its role as a sector airfield and control of the Biggin Hill Sector was passed to Hornchurch. This meant that Hornchurch's area of responsibility was extended from the Thames estuary south-eastwards to the coast, giving it temporary control over five airfields (Hornchurch, Rochford, Biggin Hill, Gravesend and Redhill) and six squadrons, with an area covering more than 5,000 square miles of sky.

Hornchurch itself did not avoid attack, there were some twenty raids against the airfield during the battle. The heaviest and most damaging occurred on 31 August when it was attacked by sixty Do17s of KG2 at 1.15 p.m. The order to scramble came too late for No. 54 Squadron and three of the eight Spitfires were hit whilst taking off. One of the pilots, Flying Officer Al Deere, crashed upside down on the airfield, but survived despite being trapped in his cockpit whilst bombs were still landing on the airfield. Pilot Officer Eric Edsall and Sergeant Jack Davis also had a lucky escape when Davis crashed into marshy ground off the end of the runway. Although there had been extensive damage, Hornchurch was fully operational again by the end of the day.

No. 41 Squadron returned to Hornchurch on 3 September, replacing No. 54 Squadron, and the Blenheims of No. 600 Squadron moved out to Redhill.

There are few better examples of the lengths that individuals would go to help others than that of Pilot Officer Peter Dexter of No. 603

Squadron. On 27 September, Pilot Officer Philip Cardell of the same squadron was badly hit during combat with Bf109s over the Channel. His attempt to bring his aircraft back over land was unsuccessful and Cardell had to bale out. He came down into the sea just short of the beach at Folkestone. In a desperate attempt to help his colleague, Peter Dexter landed his Spitfire on the beach and then commandeered a rowing boat to recover him. Unfortunately, his attempt was in vain, as Philip Cardell was already dead.

The following morning No. 41 Squadron was involved in action over Charing and lost three aircraft; one of the pilots was killed. The squadron suffered a further loss on 1 October when Bf109s shot down Pilot Officer 'Ben' Bennions over Henfield in Sussex. He managed to bale out but was badly wounded in the face and head and was taken to Queen Victoria Hospital where he became one of Archie McIndoe's 'guinea pigs'. Bennions had originally joined the squadron as a sergeant pilot in 1936 and destroyed twelve aircraft during the Battle of Britain, but the loss of an eye brought an end to his career as a fighter pilot. The squadron lost two more pilots on 11 October during combat with Bf109s over Kent, and another pilot four days later when a Bf109 of JG51 shot down Sergeant Philip Lloyd over the Channel.

On 15 October the Hornchurch operations room was moved to Lambourne Hall at Romford. There was further heavy fighting towards the end of October and Hornchurch's final casualty of the battle was Pilot Officer Alfred Davies of No. 222 Squadron, who was killed on 30 October after being shot down by Bf109s.

After the battle various squadrons made up the Hornchurch Wing, which took part in offensive operations across the Channel. During 1941 the airfield's facilities were improved to accommodate additional aircraft, including the construction of aircraft dispersal sites. The wing continued the offensive for the next three years until the V-1 rocket threat to London brought an end to wartime fighter operations as the large number of local defences in the area made air operations hazardous. For the last six months of the war Hornchurch was used as a marshalling base for personnel transiting to and from the operational theatre.

After the war the airfield was placed on care and maintenance although a reserve flying school did continue flying from it until 1953. It was then used as the RAF's Aircrew Selection Centre before the station finally closed in 1962. It was then sold and the site became a quarry and then a refuse tip. It has now been developed for housing and the Hornchurch Country Park, which covers an extensive area and is full of attractive wildlife. All the airfield's buildings have long been demolished but some reminders remain.

The site is not at first obvious in what has become a large built-up area, but it can be best found by taking the A125 Rainham to Hornchurch road northwards from the A1306. After 1 mile there is a sign for the Hornchurch Country Park to the right. After about another mile, turn right at a set of traffic lights into Airfield Way, which leads down towards the country park and marks what was once a perimeter track, following the line where the hangars once stood. The road names are all RAF-related and the road leading down to the country park is called Squadron's Approach. The car park is located in a former blast pen.

One of the local schools, the R. J. Mitchell Primary School (appropriately named after the designer of the Spitfire), can be found in Tangmere Crescent. It is situated on the former administration site and marks the area where the station headquarters once stood. In 2003 the RAF presented the local council with a Battle of Britain diptych, which contains the names of 2,000 personnel who served at

Right: One of the former blast pens is now the car park for the Hornchurch Country Park.

Below: The Hornchurch Country Park dominates the site of the former airfield.

Hornchurch and is embossed with the names of twelve surviving pilots who flew from the airfield. It is proudly displayed at Havering Town Hall, although the plan is for it to eventually be displayed in a new building on the former airfield dedicated to RAF Hornchurch.

Squadron	From	To	Aircraft	Sqn Code
65 Sqn	Start (5/6/40)	28/8/40	Spitfire	FZ
74 Sqn	Start (25/6/40)	14/8/40	Spitfire	JH
54 Sqn	24/7/40 8/8/40	28/7/40 3/9/40	Spitfire	KL
41 Sqn	26/7/40 3/9/40	8/8/40 End (23/2/41)	Spitfire	EB
266 Sqn	14/8/40	21/8/40	Spitfire	UO
264 Sqn	22/8/40	28/8/40	Defiant	PS
600 Sqn	22/8/40	12/9/40	Blenheim	BQ
603 Sqn	27/8/40	End (3/12/40)	Spitfire	XT
222 Sqn	29/8/40	End (11/11/40)	Spitfire	ZD

Summary of Squadrons at Hornchurch

Hawkinge

Hawkinge is just north of Folkestone in Kent. It was the nearest RAF station to northern France during the Battle of Britain and only ten minutes' flying time from the *Luftwaffe* airfields in the Pas-de-Calais. Its history goes back to the First World War, when the increase in air operations meant that the Royal Flying Corps needed sites that were suitable for use in the resupply of forces in France. With the shortest distance across the Channel, several sites around Dover and Folkestone were considered and land on the Downs above Folkestone was found to be suitable. Although the location of the site was at Hawkinge village, the airfield was originally known as Folkestone and was first used in early 1915 by squadrons heading across the Channel. The airfield was renamed Hawkinge during 1917 and was further developed as an aircraft acceptance park. A number of aircraft were stored there following the end of hostilities but the airfield soon became inactive and was disbanded in 1919.

During 1920 it was taken over by the RAF, and it became home to a number of fighter squadrons during the inter-war years, in particular, No. 25 Squadron from February 1920 until just before the outbreak of the Second World War. During this time the squadron operated a

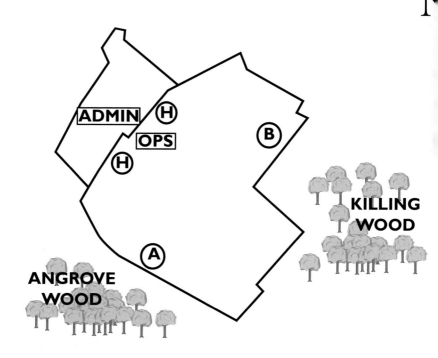

HAWKINGE – AUGUST 1940

KEY:-

Ⓐ = 'A' Flight Dispersal

Ⓑ = 'B' Flight Dispersal

OPS = Operations Block

Ⓗ = Hangars

ADMIN = Administration and Domestic Site

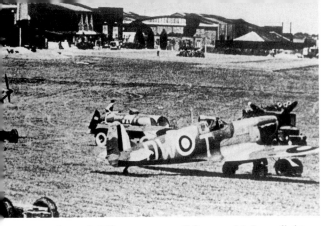

Spitfires of No. 610 Squadron at Hawkinge during July 1940.

number of different types of famous biplane fighters including the Snipe, Grebe, Siskin, Fury, Demon and Gladiator. It re-equipped with Blenheims during early 1939 but Hawkinge was not considered suitable for night operations and the airfield was transferred to Training Command. During the early months of the Second World War its location made it ideal as a listening post for monitoring German radio transmissions from across the Channel and it was not long before a number of German-speaking linguists were based in the local area.

Hawkinge was increasingly used as a forward operating airfield for No. 11 Group and as the situation deteriorated across the Channel, it was used to support the air fighting over France and the evacuation from Dunkirk. Throughout May and June preparations increased as fighter pens were constructed, the airfield was camouflaged and a number of defences were put in place.

During the first days of July the Hurricanes of No. 79 Squadron were based at Hawkinge. The squadron had just returned from France and it was amongst the first to engage heavily escorted bombers over the Channel. However, the losses that it had already suffered meant that it was moved north on the opening day of the battle for a rest. It was a further six weeks before it moved south once more to rejoin the battle.

Various squadrons used Hawkinge as a forward operating airfield during the Battle of Britain, either landing at the airfield to refuel or rearm, or operating from there on a day-by-day basis. The airfield did not have a conventional control tower but relied on two buildings to provide communications to the sector airfield at Hornchurch and to the visiting fighter squadrons. The watch office was linked to Hornchurch and a further building had a telephone link with the aircraft dispersed at two separate sites around the airfield. The domestic buildings and aircraft sheds were situated along the west and north-west boundary, near the village of Hawkinge. The aircraft dispersals were across the airfield, one ('A' Flight dispersal) in the south-west near Angrove

Wood and the second ('B' Flight dispersal) was on the eastern side near Killing Wood.

One of the more tragic events of the opening phase of the battle took place on 19 July when Defiants of No. 141 Squadron based at West Malling used Hawkinge for forward operations. The squadron was to have its first and last daylight encounter with the *Luftwaffe*. Nine Defiants scrambled soon after midday to intercept an enemy raid attacking Dover harbour. Almost immediately Bf109s of JG51 jumped them. There was no contest between the slower and less agile Defiants desperately climbing for height, and the highly capable Bf109s with height and speed on their side. During the encounter, which lasted just a minute or two, five of the nine Defiants were shot down and one crashed near Hawkinge. A seventh aircraft was hit but managed to return to base. Ten of the squadron were either killed or missing and one was wounded. The squadron had effectively been destroyed in just a matter of minutes and it was withdrawn to Scotland two days later. One of the aircraft crashed in Dover killing both the crew; one, Pilot Officer Arthur Hamilton, is buried in the cemetery next to Hawkinge airfield.

Hawkinge continued to be used by various squadrons of No. 11 Group throughout August, in particular by the Hurricanes of Nos 32 and 501 Squadrons. Typically No. 32 operated from 'A' dispersal and No. 501 from 'B' dispersal. There was often little or no warning of either an attack by enemy aircraft or a Spitfire or Hurricane making an emergency landing. This often meant having to turn a fighter round in just a matter of minutes, providing fuel and ammunition as required, or having to deal with a badly wounded pilot.

The first raid on Hawkinge took place during the late afternoon of 12 August. Damage to a number of radar sites earlier in the day meant that No. 11 Group had to ensure that a number of fighters were kept on patrols above the south-east. Whilst No. 32 Squadron was airborne over Margate, a number of Ju88s from KG76 attacked the airfield and caused significant damage. There were dozens of craters on the runway area and further damage to one of the hangars, other technical buildings and domestic accommodation. Five station personnel were killed and several more wounded. The attack happened late in the day but, despite a number of unexploded bombs and fires that had to be attended to, the airfield was ready for operations by dawn of the following day.

There was a further attack just three days later when Ju87s of LG1 attacked during the morning. One hangar was destroyed and more domestic accommodation was damaged. Later in the day He111s of KG1 and Do17s of KG2 carried out another attack but there was no more significant damage to the airfield. On 18 August Do17s attacked again but little damage was done to the airfield. More bombs were dropped on 1 September, as Hawkinge had been identified by German intelligence as a priority target. One of the hangars was hit and a number of small buildings destroyed but the airfield remained available at all times. In an attempt to confuse the *Luftwaffe* work commenced on a decoy site at nearby Wootton, 4 miles to the north of Hawkinge.

There was an unexpected visitor to the airfield during the late afternoon of 6 September. A Bf109 of LG2 force-landed at Hawkinge, having been hit by anti-aircraft fire over Chatham during an escort mission and was then attacked by RAF fighters over Canterbury. The pilot was taken prisoner.

Hawkinge was attacked again during the morning of 7 September. Bf109s and Bf110s carried out the attack from low level and a number of bombs struck various buildings, including a hangar and the officers' mess. This quick attack caused a number of casualties, including six civilians killed when a bomb hit a shelter in the village. There was one further attack on 9 October by Bf109s from low level. Although a number of buildings were hit there was no significant damage. There were a number of small-scale attacks by the occasional intruder but no significant damage. One attack on 14 October was carried out by a lone Bf109, which killed one soldier after the bomb had landed amongst the station's domestic buildings and a further attack on 27 October destroyed the officers' mess.

After the Battle of Britain was over, it was considered safe enough for a unit to be based permanently at Hawkinge. No. 421 (Reconnaissance) Flight was formed with Spitfires on 15 November and was given full squadron status as No. 91 Squadron in January 1941. Its tasks included maritime reconnaissance, shipping patrols and air-sea rescue sweeps along the Channel.

During the summer of 1942 the airfield was used by Spitfires to carry out offensive operations across the Channel and these were later replaced by more powerful Spitfires during 1943 to counter the *Luftwaffe*'s FW190, which was causing continuous problems along the south-east coast. Spitfires from several different squadrons used Hawkinge during the latter half of 1943 and the early months of 1944, and Spitfires enjoyed some success against the German V-1 rockets during the summer of 1944. The airfield was also used by severely damaged bombers returning from operations, as well as being used by the Fleet Air Arm to deny the German navy ships and U-boats any freedom either in the Channel or the waters off the south-east coast of England. There was also a dedicated flight of two Lysanders and two Walrus amphibians, which carried out air-sea rescue duties from 1941 until the squadron disbanded in February 1945.

At the end of the Second World War Hawkinge was placed on care and maintenance and was then transferred to Technical Training Command. In 1949 the Women's Royal Air Force (WRAF) was formed and Hawkinge became its depot. Following a brief period as the WRAF's Officer Cadets Training Unit, reorganization resulted in Hawkinge once again being placed on care and maintenance in 1961. The site was used during filming of *The Battle of Britain* in 1968, after which the land reverted to pasture. Although many buildings were demolished, some survived and were used for a variety of purposes during the 1970s and 1980s. Barrack accommodation was turned into flats and the officers' mess became a hostel. A Spitfire once stood proudly at the main gate but was removed before the station was finally closed.

The site has now largely been developed for housing as the area has undergone one of the largest residential development programmes in the south-east of England. However, the history of the airfield has been preserved by the Kent Battle of Britain Museum, which has been established on the site. It can be found by taking the A20 Dover to Folkestone road, and turning north towards Canterbury on the A260; it is signposted. After 1 mile, in the village of Hawkinge, turn left into Aerodrome Road. After less than a mile the entrance to the former camp is on the left and the former gymnasium still stands, although it is not used. Outside the gymnasium there is a small monument with the words 'This monument was erected to commemorate the part played by the Royal Air Force Station Hawkinge in the air defence of Great Britain 1915–61 and to provide a memorial to all who served at or flew from this green swath never to return.' There is also a quote from Winston Churchill in 1940: 'History with its flickering lamp stumbles along the trail of the past trying to reconstruct its scenes to revive its echoes and kindle with pale gleams the passion of former days.' The monument includes the original compass-swinging circle taken from the concrete floor of one of the hangars and was dedicated in 1978.

Just a few hundred yards past the monument there is a turning to the left to the Kent Battle of Britain Museum. It is entirely self-supporting and stands or falls by the number of visitors it attracts. It is run by a

106

The Kent Battle of Britain Museum is situated in some original 1940 buildings on the historic airfield at Hawkinge.

small number of volunteers and enthusiasts. The museum has a number of original 1940 buildings, some of which still bear the scars of war. It was opened to the public in 1971 and contains the world's largest collection of Battle of Britain relics and related memorabilia. The largest building is the Stuart-Buttle Memorial Hangar, which was opened by his widow in 1995 and contains full-sized replicas of Hurricanes and Spitfires and vehicles that would have been found on an airfield in 1940. The Dowding Memorial Hangar, which was erected in tribute to Air Chief Marshal Sir Hugh Dowding, contains replica aircraft that were used in the film *The Battle of Britain* and parts of Bf109s recovered from the battle. The former operations block is now home to items gleaned from over 600 Battle of Britain aircraft, the majority of which were excavated by the museum's recovery team in the 1960s and 1970s, or have been donated by individuals since the

A monument to commemorate the part played by Hawkinge in the defence of Great Britain can be found just outside the old gymnasium in Aerodrome Road.

foundation of the collection. The fourth building is the original 'B' Flight dispersal hut, which now houses one of the museum's two V-1 flying bombs. The fifth is the original armoury, which contains a comprehensive collection of weaponry, uniforms and personal items donated to the museum.

The opening times of the museum are from Easter Friday to 30 September, Tuesday to Sunday from 10.00 a.m. to 5.00 p.m. Last admission is at 4.00 p.m. The museum is closed on Mondays, except Bank Holidays, and is closed from October to Easter. Admission for adults is £3.50, for Seniors £3 and for children £2. There is free parking for cars and coaches, and there is a shop and refreshments for sale. On the grounds of both security and copyright, the museum regrets that no cameras, video recorders, notebooks or any other types of recording equipment are allowed. The address is: Kent Battle of Britain Museum, Aerodrome Road, Hawkinge Airfield, Near Folkestone, Kent, CT18 7AG. Telephone: 01303 893140 or e-mail: kentbattleofbritainmuseum@btinternet.com.

Continuing past the museum, it is possible to drive around parts of the former airfield. After the museum turn left into Elvington Lane and the officers' mess is on the right. After a short distance take the next left into Gibraltar Lane where some of the original aircraft blast pens can be found. It is also a good point from which to look across the site. Continuing along Gibraltar Lane the airfield's close proximity to the cliffs and sea soon becomes obvious. In addition to air attacks the area was also shelled from across the Channel by long-range artillery, and it is easy to understand why the area became known as 'Hellfire Corner'.

Sqn (home base in brackets)	Aircraft	Sqn Code
79 Squadron (Biggin Hill)	Hurricane	AL
141 Squadron (West Malling)	Defiant	TW
32 Squadron (Biggin Hill)	Hurricane	KT
501 Squadron (Gravesend)	Hurricane	SD
615 Squadron (Kenley)	Hurricane	KW
111 Squadron (Croydon)	Hurricane	TM
72 Squadron (Croydon)	Spitfire	RN
610 Squadron (Biggin Hill)	Spitfire	DW

Squadrons known to have operated from Hawkinge
during the Battle of Britain

Above: The former officer's mess at Hawkinge can be found in Elvington Lane.

Left: Some of the original fighter blast pens have survived at Hawkinge and can be found in Gibraltar Lane on the western side of the airfield.

Manston

Located 2 miles west of Ramsgate on the Isle of Thanet, Manston airfield dates back to the First World War when the Zeppelin airships appeared in 1915, which meant that the Royal Naval Air Service required more landing grounds in the south-east. A large field was found to be suitable on the western side of Ramsgate and was developed during 1916, with a hangar and permanent buildings. During 1917 part of the pilot training school at Eastchurch was transferred to Manston and the Admiralty then selected it as one of the two main instructional units for the Royal Naval Air Service (the other being at Cranwell in Lincolnshire).

The end of the war brought a reduction in flying activity but the large number of technical buildings made Manston an ideal location for technical training. In 1919, therefore, the School of Technical Training moved there from Halton. Flying activity resumed in 1921, with Manston being used for pilot refresher training prior to deployment overseas. In 1924 Bristol Fighters of No. 2 Squadron arrived and were soon joined by Vickers Vimys of No. 9 Squadron. These two squadrons served together at Manston until the end of 1930.

During the mid-1930s Manston was home to the School of Air Navigation and No. 3 School of Technical Training. The RAF's expansion scheme meant that it required large numbers of aircrew and the establishment at Manston increased during 1936. During the final months before the Second World War, the School of Air Navigation moved out and the School of Technical Training dispersed. The station was transferred to Fighter Command in November 1939 and during the spring of 1940 was used by squadrons providing fighter cover across the Channel in support of ground forces in France and then over Dunkirk during the evacuation.

Manston was used as a forward operating airfield for No. 11 Group during the Battle of Britain; the only permanent residents were the Blenheims of No. 600 Squadron. It was an all-grass airfield with no constructed runways. Generally, up to three squadrons at a time would use it daily to relieve the main bases. Life there during the early days of the battle was somewhat routine, as initially the squadrons just flew protective patrols over the Channel.

No. 41 Squadron was operating from Manston during the morning of 29 July when it intercepted a number of Ju87s and Bf109s in the Dover area and Flying Officer Douglas Gamblen was shot down and killed. No. 600 Squadron suffered its first loss on 8 August when a Bf109 of JG26 shot down one of its Blenheims off Ramsgate. Flying Officer Dennis Grice, Sergeant Francis Keast and AC1 John Warren were all killed. Witnesses reported that Grice had deliberately remained at the controls of the burning aircraft to avoid the town of Ramsgate.

On 12 August Manston received a devastating attack. Spitfires of No. 65 Squadron were detached from Hornchurch and soon after midday Bf110s of *Erprobungsgruppe* 210 appeared from nowhere and dropped bombs and strafed the aircraft and buildings. At the same time Do17s of KG2 carried out a bombing attack from medium level and there was significant damage to the airfield. A Spitfire was damaged as it tried to take off during the attack, although Pilot Officer Ken Hart had a lucky escape and survived. Two Blenheims of No. 600 Squadron were also damaged during the attack but no one was hurt. Two hangars were badly damaged, other buildings were destroyed and the runway was left cratered. This damage convinced German intelligence that

Manston had been completely destroyed but it had not, and was back ready for operations again by the following day.

Two days later the same happened again. It was just after midday when the same Bf110s of *Erprobungsgruppe* 210 returned, but this time the attack was even more devastating. Three Blenheims of No. 600 Squadron were completely destroyed and four hangars were badly damaged. However, local defences brought down two of the Bf110s; one was hit by anti-aircraft fire and crashed at Manston with both crew killed, and the second collided with another and also crashed at Manston; one of the crew was killed and the other was taken prisoner.

The low-level attacks continued daily, which caused more damage to Manston and an increasing number of casualties. The situation became desperate; there was little or no water and few buildings could be used. Meals had to be taken wherever and whenever possible in between the raids. The situation reached an all-time low soon after midday on 24 August when the airfield received yet another attack. Several bombs fell on it and many buildings were destroyed. Seven people were killed. There then followed a second attack, which struck just as quickly as the first. There was more damage to many buildings and domestic accommodation and all communications with the sector airfield at Hornchurch and HQ No. 11 Group were lost.

In addition to the damage on the ground, there was devastation for the Defiants of No. 264 Squadron, which had been ordered from its base at Hornchurch to provide air cover over Manston. One section was in the air and the other on the ground to refuel. There was little warning of the raid; the crews rushed to their aircraft and were taking to the air as the bombs started to fall. It was the worst possible time for the Defiants, as they had little speed and no height. Three were immediately shot down and one more was lost in the following few minutes. Six of the aircrew were killed and one later died of his wounds. The squadron suffered further during the following five days. Between 24 and 28 August it lost ten aircraft destroyed with fourteen of the squadron's aircrew killed or missing. It was the end for the Defiants as day fighters and what was left of the squadron returned to Lincolnshire.

The damage caused during these attacks meant that the airfield had to be abandoned and could only be used as an emergency landing ground. The Blenheims of No. 600 Squadron were withdrawn from Manston and moved further back to Hornchurch, where they would have more warning of attack. The station personnel dispersed to a number of buildings in the local area, the majority moving to Westgate-on-Sea on the western side of Margate. Winston Churchill visited Manston on 28 August to witness the damage and ongoing work to get the airfield ready for operations once more.

Following hard work, Manston was available for use by early September. On the 5th No. 41 Squadron lost four Spitfires during the afternoon action over the Thames estuary. Two of the pilots were killed when they collided during an attack against Do17s, including the squadron's commanding officer, Squadron Leader Hilary Hood. The other was one of the squadron's flight commanders, Flight Lieutenant John Webster, who had been with the squadron since the outbreak of the war and had already destroyed eleven enemy aircraft, including two Bf109s just before the mid-air collision. Although he managed to bale out, he fell dead to the ground. Command of No. 41 Squadron was passed to Squadron Leader Robert Lister, but he remained for just a few days before a Bf109 shot him down on 14 September. He survived but was replaced by Squadron Leader Donald Finlay.

Wing Commander Graham Manton took command of Manston at the beginning of September, having been promoted following his command of No. 56 Squadron at North Weald. As the *Luftwaffe* turned its efforts away from the airfields of No. 11 Group, there was just the occasional hit on Manston, without any further serious damage. The only other German visitor before the end of the battle was a Bf109 of JG53, which crash-landed at Manston following combat with Spitfires over the Thames estuary during the afternoon of 17 October; the pilot survived and was taken prisoner.

Manston was used by a number of squadrons in a variety of roles during the months after the Battle of Britain. In February 1942, the Fleet Air Arm used it during its heroic attempt to stop the German battleships *Scharnhorst* and *Gneisenau* breaking out of the French port of Brest and passing through the Dover Straits. Spitfires of the North Weald Wing later used it as a forward operating base for offensive operations across the Channel. It was also used as an emergency airfield by badly damaged bombers of Bomber Command and the USAAF. Several squadrons and detachments continued to use it as its location made it an ideal operating base for raids across the Channel. In April 1943 Barnes Wallis used it for trials of his bouncing bomb, code-named 'Highball', in preparation for the attack against the dams in Germany.

Because of Manston's location as an emergency airfield, work to extend the runway began in June 1943. It was extended to 3,000 yards long, and a large dispersal loop and crash bays were constructed, but it was nearly a year before work was completed. After the war there was little use for the airfield by Fighter Command and it was taken over by Transport Command in 1946. The Americans subsequently used it from 1950 before it became a master diversion airfield in 1956. This meant that it had to remain open twenty-four hours a day, 365 days a year, to receive any aircraft with an emergency. In 1958 it was returned to Fighter Command and placed on care and maintenance before it was reopened the following year as a master diversion airfield for No. 11 Group.

Many different bodies, including civilian organizations, used Manston at some time or another during the 1960s and 1970s. Among them were the fire service and HM Customs. Civil aviation companies started using the airfield during the 1960s and it was home to RAF search and rescue helicopters from 1961 until RAF Manston closed in 1999. However, the civil part of the airfield remained and has now become Kent International Airport.

The site dominates the Isle of Thanet and can be found by taking the A229 and then the A259 towards Ramsgate; it is well signposted. The runway is situated between the A259 and B2190. Incidentally, the A259 follows the line of the old southern taxiway close to the main runway and the B2190 cuts across the old RAF station. There are some original buildings left, including the southernmost hangar on the western side, which was there during the Battle of Britain, and an original black hangar dating back to 1918, which is situated near the original site of the old watch office.

By following the B2190 around the northern side of the runway, you pass through the main site and there is much of historical interest to be found. The Spitfire and Hurricane Memorial Building was first opened in June 1981 to house Spitfire TB752 and was the very first building to be erected on any RAF station to house a gate-guardian aircraft.

The adjoining part of the building, which houses Hurricane LF751, was opened in October 1988. The Memorial Building also houses the superb Battle of Britain Tapestry and a collection of memorabilia,

Left: The Allied Aircrew Memorial and the Spitfire and Hurricane Memorial Building at Manston.

Below: Looking south through the Allied Air Forces Memorial Garden down the line of where the original runway used to run. RAF Manston finally closed in 1999 and the site has now become Kent International Airport.

much of which relates to the Battle of Britain. Outside the building is the Allied Aircrew Memorial, which was unveiled by Her Majesty Queen Elizabeth the Queen Mother on 18 July 1997. There is also the Allied Air Forces Memorial Garden overlooking the main airfield. No charge is made for admission but as it is totally self-funding donations are most welcome. The members of staff are all volunteers and are most helpful. There is free car parking and refreshments are available at the Merlin Cafeteria. There is also provision for wheelchair users. The Memorial Building is open throughout the year (except 25–27 December inclusive and 1 January). Opening times are from 10.00 a.m. to 5.00 p.m. from April to September and from 10.00 a.m. to 4.00 p.m. from October to March. The address is: The Spitfire and Hurricane Memorial Building, Manston, Ramsgate, Kent, CT12 5DF. Telephone/Fax: 01843 821940 or e-mail: www.spitfire-museum.com. The Memorial Building is signposted from the A259.

At the same location there is also the RAF Manston History Museum next to the Memorial Building, which is open daily from 10.00 a.m. Admission is £1 for adults and free for under-16s. Further along the road, on the left opposite the Air Traffic Control Tower, is the MoD Fire Services Central Training Establishment.

Squadron	From	To	Aircraft	Sqn Code
600 Sqn	Start (20/6/40)	22/8/40	Blenheim	BQ

Summary of Manston

Gravesend

Although geographically located in the Hornchurch Sector, Gravesend was used during the Battle of Britain as a satellite airfield for Biggin Hill. Its history dates back to the early 1930s, when the increased popularity of flying and the expansion of commercial aviation led to the development of the site. Although Croydon was London's main airport, Gravesend quickly became established as an alternative airfield on the eastern side of London when landing at Croydon was not possible. Although located on the Thames estuary, the fact that the airfield was some 250 ft above sea level made Gravesend ideal for development because it generally remained free of fog.

The airfield lay east of Gravesend, south of Chalk village, and was home to several aircraft and commercial companies during the 1930s. The RAF first made use of it in 1933 during exercises. When the Second World War began it was taken over by the Air Ministry to

115

Blenheim Ifs of No. 604 Squadron at Gravesend during July 1940.

become a satellite station for Biggin Hill. There were also two decoy airfields at nearby Cliffe to the north-east and Luddesdown to the south-east.

Gravesend was used by several squadron detachments during the opening months of the war. When the Battle of Britain began it was home to the Blenheims of No. 604 Squadron. The squadron flew night patrols but without any contact and was replaced at the end of July by the Hurricanes of No. 501 Squadron. Within two days this squadron was in action when, on 29 July, it engaged a large number of Ju87s escorted by Bf109s. It claimed six enemy aircraft destroyed and a further six damaged. One pilot to claim a Ju87 during the encounter was Sergeant Donald McKay. It was one of his eight kills whilst at Gravesend, for which he was awarded the DFM.

During the early days of the battle the normal procedure for the squadron's pilots was to deploy to the forward airfield at Hawkinge at first light. They would then operate from there during the day and

return to Gravesend at last light. However, things did not always go to plan and the increased number of air attacks against Hawkinge meant that the squadron had to operate from Gravesend for extensive periods during August.

Another successful pilot during this period was Sergeant 'Ginger' Lacey who scored nine of his victories operating from Gravesend and whilst

'Ginger' Lacey who scored nine of his eventual twenty-eight victories whilst serving with No. 501 Squadron at Gravesend during the Battle of Britain and was the RAF's top scoring pilot during the battle.

deployed to Hawkinge. These successes brought his total to fifteen confirmed kills. During the second half of August alone, he destroyed five enemy aircraft for which he was awarded the DFM. He was undoubtedly one of the finest to have flown from Gravesend during the battle and he went on to become the RAF's highest scoring pilot during the Battle of Britain.

Gravesend suffered its first attack on 2 September. Although it was bombed, there was little damage and just two personnel were wounded. No. 501 Squadron lost one Hurricane when it failed to return from combat over Dungeness. Flying Officer Arthur Rose-Price had only joined the squadron that morning; he was twenty-one years old. On 4 September bombs fell once again but only in the vicinity of the airfield. Two days later there were further losses for No. 501 Squadron when three pilots were killed during combat over Ashford.

The Hurricanes of No. 501 Squadron moved to Kenley on 10 September to change places with the Spitfires of No. 66 Squadron, which moved into Gravesend the following day. The squadron was immediately in action during the late afternoon. One successful pilot during the squadron's time at Gravesend was Flight Lieutenant Bobby Oxspring. The son of a decorated Royal Flying Corps pilot, who had served also with No. 66 Squadron during the First World War, Bobby Oxspring was just twenty-one years old during the Battle of Britain. Whilst at Gravesend he destroyed eight enemy aircraft and was awarded the DFC. Six of his kills were during September. On the 11th he destroyed an He111 east of Rye, which was followed by a Do17 south of Chatham on the 15th, a Bf109 near Hawkinge on the 18th, an He111 near Hastings on the 24th, a Bf110 over Kent on the 27th and a Bf109 near Biggin Hill on the 30th.

On 4 October the squadron lost one of its flight commanders, Flight Lieutenant Ken Gillies who, whilst serving at Gravesend, had destroyed one enemy aircraft and shared in the destruction of at least five others. The circumstances of his death are not clear. He was scrambled with two others to intercept a lone He111 over the Hastings-Dungeness area but did not return; his body was eventually washed ashore in Suffolk.

At the age of just twenty-one years old, Flight Lieutenant Bobby Oxspring served with No. 66 Squadron at Gravesend during the Battle of Britain. He was awarded the DFC after destroying eight enemy aircraft.

No. 66 Squadron remained at Gravesend until the end of the battle and was joined by No. 421 Flight, which formed at Gravesend on 7 October. The flight was essentially formed with personnel from No. 66 Squadron and was given the special role of patrolling high above the Channel in order to report any large build-up of enemy aircraft. This was a visual form of airborne early warning, although the flight did not escape engagements with the enemy. On 11 October one of its pilots was killed during combat over Hawkinge. Sergeant Charles Ayling had already served with Nos 43 and 66 Squadrons during the battle. His Spitfire crashed at Newchurch. There were several more incidents involving No. 421 Flight and enemy fighters but no more pilots were lost during the battle.

The facilities at Gravesend were improved after the Battle of Britain and it became a fully functioning station. By 1943, the runways had been lengthened and facilities improved such that three squadrons could operate from it at any one time. It remained a busy fighter station until D-Day and the subsequent break-out from Normandy. The V-1 attacks against London during the summer of 1944 brought flying there to a temporary halt as the airfield was in the V-1's line of attack. It was declared non-operational and heavy balloons appeared in the sky all around. Its role then switched to that of local control for the aircraft in the vicinity, to keep them clear of all the local defences.

At the end of the war the airfield was put on care and maintenance. Essex Aero remained there until 1956, when it closed and a large

A plaque to commemorate the fifteen pilots killed whilst serving at Gravesend during the Battle of Britain is proudly displayed in the entrance to Cascades Leisure Centre on the site of the former airfield.

housing estate was built on the site. There are no obvious signs of the former airfield and the site is now the Riverview Park housing estate and a sports complex with a golf course. In the entrance to the Cascades Leisure Centre is a plaque containing the names of the fifteen pilots who were killed whilst operating from Gravesend during the Battle of Britain.

The site can be found by taking the A2 from the M25 towards Rochester. Continue past the turn-off to Gravesend East and, about 2 miles before the A2 becomes the M2, take the road off to the left to the village of Thong. After about 3 miles, and having passed through the village, the golf course can be seen on the right and a housing estate on the left. This is the site of the former airfield and the turning into the Leisure Centre is on the right.

Squadron	From	To	Aircraft	Sqn Code
604 Sqn	Start (3/7/40)	26/7/40	Blenheim	NG
501 Sqn	25/7/40	10/9/40	Hurricane	SD
66 Sqn	11/9/40	30/10/40	Spitfire	RB/LZ
421 Flight	7/10/40	30/10/40	Hurricane Spitfire	L-Z

Summary of Squadrons at Gravesend

Rochford

Rochford was another airfield located in the Hornchurch Sector but was used by another sector; in this case, it was a satellite for North Weald for all but the opening days of the Battle of Britain. Its history goes back to the First World War. Owing to its proximity to Southend, it was initially referred to as either Southend or Rochford, and sometimes as Eastwood. It was first used for military purposes when the Admiralty selected a number of landing grounds to counter the Zeppelin raids on London in 1915. However, there was little flying activity and changes in responsibilities led to it being transferred to the Royal Flying Corps in 1916. Work began to develop the site, but there was still little flying during 1916. It was home to various units of the Royal Flying Corps before it was taken over by the newly formed RAF in 1918. Development of the station was completed with the construction of four large hangars, as well as technical and domestic buildings. However, the end of the First World War brought a rapid reduction in activity and the station was closed in 1920, with the land reverting to agriculture.

The popularity of aviation led to it being reopened in 1935. It was mostly used by Southend Flying Club but there were also various air displays and other rallies during the years leading up to the Second World War. In the final build-up to war, all airfields and land were inspected for suitability for the RAF and Rochford became a forward satellite for Hornchurch. Spitfires of Nos 54 and 74 Squadrons, and Blenheims of No. 600 Squadron were all regular users of the airfield during the opening weeks of the war.

When the Battle of Britain began the airfield was home to the Spitfires of No. 54 Squadron. During the morning of 24 July the squadron intercepted a formation of Do17s bombing a Channel convoy off Dover. Later that day it was in action with Bf109s of JG26 over Margate. Flying Officer Johnny Allen was killed whilst attempting to reach Manston after his Spitfire had suffered engine damage, and he crashed at Cliftonville. He had made the squadron's first claim of the war when he shot down a Ju88 in the Dunkirk area on 21 May, and he was credited with seven enemy aircraft destroyed and awarded the DFC. He is buried in the Margate Cemetery in Kent.

On 25 July No. 54 Squadron was again in action whilst protecting a convoy in the Channel during the afternoon. Led by Flight Lieutenant Basil 'Wonky' Way the squadron engaged a large formation of Ju87s, escorted by Bf109s, which were attacking the convoy. Way destroyed one Bf109 before he was shot down and killed by another. He had been with the squadron since before the war and had been a flight commander since May 1940. At the time of his death he was twenty-two years old. His body was eventually washed ashore across the Channel and he was buried in Belgium. Later on the same day the squadron suffered a further loss when a Bf109 shot down and killed Pilot Officer Archie Finnie over the Channel. He is buried in Margate Cemetery in Kent.

No. 54 Squadron left Rochford on 24 July and the airfield was then used as a satellite for North Weald for the rest of the Battle of Britain. There were few luxuries at the site; the main squadron facility centred on a large bell tent with a field telephone linked to the North Weald operations room. The Hurricanes of No. 56 Squadron soon became regular visitors and detachments would often operate from the site to ease the burden on its home base of North Weald.

When the *Luftwaffe* turned its attention to the airfields of No. 11 Group, Rochford initially escaped attack. However, on the morning of 25 August thirty He111s of KG53 got through the air defences and attacked the airfield but caused little damage. Later in the day thirty

Do17s of KG3 attacked it from medium level, causing damage to several building and leaving craters across the runway area. However, the damage did not prevent the airfield from remaining operational, which proved lucky for one Do17 crew of KG2 during the afternoon of the following day. It had been taking part in an attack on Hornchurch when it was attacked by RAF fighters and suffered severe damage. With little alternative it had to make a forced-landing at Rochford and the crew were taken prisoner.

The Defiants of No. 264 Squadron moved in to Rochford on 27 August. This unit had suffered appalling losses during the previous few days and was taken out of the battle and moved north back to Lincolnshire the following day. It did, however, return briefly at the end of the battle as a night-fighter unit.

Rochford was attacked again on 28 August, although most of the bombs fell in the local vicinity. The airfield was, however, left cratered and suffered the loss of communications.

In similar circumstances to those of 26 August, a Do17 of KG3 crash-landed on the airfield on 2 September, having been badly damaged by Hurricanes of No. 249 Squadron over Chatham. Three of the crew survived and were taken prisoner but the rear gunner was killed. Apart from these isolated incidents the airfield was spared any large-scale attacks during the battle. The reasons for this might be that German intelligence did not consider it a priority airfield as it was not one of No. 11 Group's main operating bases. It was also situated on the northern side of the Thames estuary and just that bit further than other forward operating airfields such as Manston or Hawkinge.

At the end of the battle the airfield was upgraded as a night-fighter station and renamed RAF Southend. It reverted to daytime operations in 1941 and many of No. 11 Group's squadrons used it for offensive

Defiant of No. 264 Squadron at Rochford.

operations across the Channel. There were occasional attacks by the *Luftwaffe* in an attempt to disrupt operations.

In 1942 Lysanders arrived as target-towing aircraft to provide the squadrons of No. 11 Group with air-to-air gunnery practice, and the airfield was home to Americans of No. 121 'Eagle' Squadron, Belgians of No. 350 Squadron and Australians of No. 453 (RAAF) Squadron at various times during 1942 and 1943. These squadrons were equipped with Spitfires and flew various types of sorties, ranging from mission sweeps across France to coastal patrols. The role of the station changed during 1943 with the departure of the Spitfires and it became increasingly used for armament training. In 1944 it briefly reverted to its original status as a satellite airfield for Hornchurch before it was placed on care and maintenance and finally closed in May 1946.

Its close proximity to both Southend and London meant that the airfield was a useful site for post-war development and it became a civil airport in 1947, with various commercial operators using it throughout the 1950s and 1960s. Plans to extend the runway and provide facilities for the new jet airliners did not come to fruition, however, and as a result of competition from sea ferry companies the 1970s saw the gradual demise of cargo and passenger services.

There was a period when it looked as though the airfield would be closed to commercial operators, but it survived and during the 1980s it was rated the UK's fourth busiest in terms of aircraft movements. London Southend Airport, as it is now called, has been owned by Regional Airports Limited since 1994 and is currently expanding in the expectation of handling up to 300,000 passengers a year.

The airport is 18 miles from Junction 29 of the M25, just to the north of the A127 at Southend and can be found by taking the A1159

The former airfield of Rochford is now Southend Airport.

towards Rochford. The best way to view the airfield is by taking the Eastern Boundary Road, which can be found at the Harp House Roundabout. The address is: London Southend Airport, Southend-on-Sea, Essex, SS2 6YF. Telephone: 01702 608100.

Squadron	From	To	Aircraft	Sqn Code
54 Sqn	Start (25/6/40)	24/7/40	Spitfire	KL
264 Sqn	27/8/40 29/10/40	28/8/40 End (27/11/40)	Defiant	PS

Summary of Squadrons at Rochford

Detling

Detling is just to the north-east of Maidstone in Kent and dates back to 1915, when both the Royal Naval Air Service and the Royal Flying Corps first used the airfield during the First World War. After the war it closed and became farmland until the 1930s, when it was redeveloped as part of the RAF's expansion scheme. It was initially used by Bomber Command, but was transferred to Coastal Command in 1938.

Detling was actively involved during operations over France in the spring of 1940 and the subsequent evacuation from Dunkirk, and was home to Ansons of No. 500 Squadron and Blenheims of No. 53 Squadron during the Battle of Britain. Both squadrons remained at the airfield throughout the battle although neither is officially recognized as having participated in the Battle of Britain.

Detling was considered important enough by German intelligence to be counted as one of their priority airfields for attack and it suffered a heavy bombardment during the afternoon of 13 August when more than fifty Ju87s of LG1, escorted by Bf109s of JG26, attacked, causing significant damage to the airfield's runways and hangars. Furthermore, more than twenty aircraft were destroyed or seriously damaged on the ground, mainly Ansons but also eight Blenheims of No. 53 Squadron. The operations room received a direct hit, with the tragic loss of the station commander, Group Captain Edward Davis. More than sixty of the station's personnel were killed during the attack and a further 100 wounded.

Every attempt was made to disperse the aircraft and personnel, but there were further attacks between 30 August and 2 September. In particular the damage caused by thirty Do17s on 2 September proved significant and the airfield was out of action for a number of hours. A

Hurricane of No. 111 Squadron had to make a forced landing there following damage caused whilst attacking He111s over the Thames estuary; unfortunately for the pilot, Flight Lieutenant Herbert Giddings, he landed during an attack but he managed to survive.

The airfield no longer exists. The site is now used as the Kent County Showground, but there are a few reminders of former days, such as concrete pill boxes. It can be found by taking the A249 from Junction 7 of the M20 at Maidstone, towards Sheerness. After just over 2 miles, it is on the left and access to the site is possible.

The former airfield at Detling is now the Kent County Showground.

Eastchurch

Although a Coastal Command airfield and not very often used by No. 11 Group during the Battle of Britain, Eastchurch suffered badly during the summer of 1940. The reasons for this are not particularly obvious, as its location makes it unlikely that the *Luftwaffe* bomber crews would have confused it with other airfields in the area. It is more likely that German intelligence thought it was being used more than it actually was or that continuous bombing of the airfield would prevent its use during the battle.

Located on the Isle of Sheppey just to the south of the A250, Eastchurch is one of the oldest sites in British aviation history. It was first used in 1909 and then by the Royal Aero Club in 1910. It was then developed into a large air station for the Royal Naval Air Service during the First World War. During the Second World War it was used by Coastal Command to carry out raids against German shipping and the invasion barges concentrating in occupied ports across the Channel.

On 12 August the Spitfires of No. 266 Squadron moved in with the Fairey Battles of Nos 12 and 142 Squadrons. The next day the airfield was attacked by more than fifty Do17s of KG2, during the early morning confusion of 13 August, the opening day of *Adler tag*. The Dorniers were picked up by radar but it was unclear what their target might be. The weather in the Eastchurch area was cloudy but there were gaps through which the airfield could be seen by the attackers. Although Spitfires from No. 74 Squadron spotted them above the cloud at 10,000 ft, their interception came too late. On the ground there had been no warning and the result was devastating. Several aircraft were either destroyed or damaged. The operations block took a direct hit and fourteen of the station personnel were killed and a further thirty wounded. The raiders, however, did not escape without loss; five Do17s were shot down and a further seven returned to their bases damaged.

The damage to the airfield meant that the Spitfires of No. 266 Squadron moved out to Hornchurch the following day and the Battles were carefully dispersed, as were the station's personnel. There were further attacks against the airfield in early September, which caused significant damage and put Eastchurch out of action for much of September. The Battles were withdrawn north.

After the war the airfield was transferred to the Prison Commissioners. Today it is a prison complex with HMP Standford Hill (an open prison) on the main site and HMP Swaleside and HMP Elmley (secure prisons) on the opposite side of the road.

The site can be found by taking the A249 onto the Isle of Sheppey. Before Sheerness, take the B2231 towards Leysdown. At the roundabout just before the village of Eastchurch, bear right and continue towards Leysdown. At the next mini-roundabout turn right towards the prisons and the road takes you through the site, with the former airfield off to the right. Photography in the area is prohibited.

Of related interest in the village of Eastchurch is an attractive memorial to the early pioneers of aviation. It can be found by retracing your route from the prisons and crossing the B2231 into the village of Eastchurch. The memorial is situated about $\frac{1}{2}$ mile on the left, in the village centre, opposite All Saints Parish Church.

Capel-le-Ferne

The National Memorial to the Battle of Britain at Capel-le-Ferne is a place that anyone interested in the battle should take time to visit. It is a magnificent monument on the east side of Folkestone overlooking East Wear Bay and the Straits of Dover. On a clear day the coast of France can be seen quite clearly. It can be found on the B2011, at the village of Capel-le-Ferne, just to the south of the A20 Dover to Folkestone road.

The memorial was the idea of the former Battle of Britain pilot, Wing Commander Geoffrey Page, who suggested that there should be a permanent national Battle of Britain memorial. It occupies a commanding position on the cliffs overlooking the Channel. The design is based on a large three-bladed propeller with a stone figure of a seated pilot looking out across the Channel. On the sandstone base are carved the squadron badges of all the squadrons that took part in the Battle of Britain. The memorial was unveiled by Her Majesty Queen Elizabeth the Queen Mother on 9 July 1993.

At the same site there is also the Beaverbrook Wall, which was completed in 1999 and donated by the Beaverbrook Foundation 'in memory of Group Captain The Honourable Max Aitken DSO DFC, No. 601 Squadron Battle of Britain 1940'. The wall bears the famous words of the Prime Minister, Winston Churchill, 'Never in the field of human conflict was so much owed by so many to so few.' Opposite the wall is the Millenium Creative Brickwork, which was completed in 2000 to mark the 60th anniversary of the Battle of Britain. It was designed and constructed by the staff and students of the South Kent College.

A masthead, which was originally at Biggin Hill, flies the RAF ensign. On each side of it are ten flags representing the nationalities of those other countries whose pilots flew in the Battle of Britain: Australia, Belgium, Canada, Czechoslovakia, the Free French, Ireland, New Zealand, Poland, South Africa and the USA. At the foot of the masthead is a black labrador called 'BOB' (Battle of Britain), which represents the squadron mascot. There is also a full-sized replica of a Hurricane at the site, which is in the markings of 'US-X' as flown by Pilot Officer Geoffrey Page when he was shot down and badly burned on 12 August 1940 whilst serving with No. 56 Squadron at North Weald. The plan is for it to be joined by a replica of a Spitfire in the markings of No. 72 Squadron, as flown by Pilot Officer Herbert Case when he was killed on 12 August 1940. His aircraft crashed at Capel-le-Ferne just to the north of the memorial.

The site can be visited at any time, although the visitor's centre is open daily from 1 April to 30 September from 11.00 a.m. to 5.00 p.m. There is ample free car parking and the centre provides refreshments and souvenirs, with facilities for the disabled. Further information can be obtained during opening hours by telephone on 01303 249292 or after hours on 01732 870809. Each year a Memorial Day is held around the weekend of 10 July, the opening day of the Battle of Britain, and is attended by veterans and guests. An organization called 'Friends of the Few' formed in 2001 and supports the work of the Battle of Britain Memorial Trust with the aim of preserving the memory of those who served during the Battle of Britain. Membership costs £25 per year and more details can be obtained from the Secretary of the Battle of Britain Memorial Trust, Group Captain Patrick Tootal, at 4 The Croft, Leybourne, West Malling, Kent, ME19 5QD. Tel: 01732 870809.

The National Monument to the Battle of Britain at Capel-le-Ferne. The design is based on a three-bladed propeller with a stone figure of a seated pilot overlooking the Channel. On the sandstone base is carved the badges of all the squadrons that took part in the Battle of Britain.

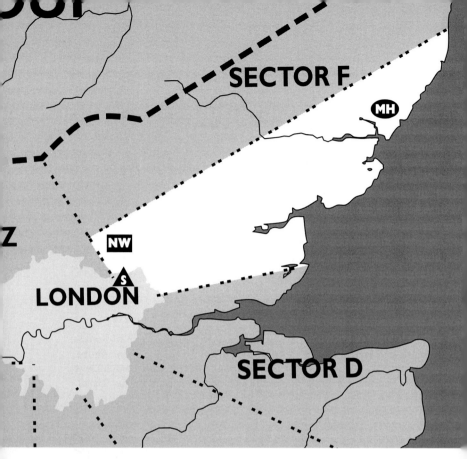

SECTOR E – AUGUST 1940

KEY:-

NW = North Weald, Sector Airfield

S = Stapleford Tawney, Satellite Airfield

MH = Martlesham Heath, Forward Operating Airfield

CHAPTER SEVEN

NORTH WEALD SECTOR
SECTOR E

The North Weald Sector, or Sector E, covered the area to the north-east of London and had three airfields. Its southern boundary, to the east of London, was with the Hornchurch Sector just to the north of the Thames estuary, and it was bounded to the north by the Debden Sector. The sector airfield was North Weald itself, which had a satellite airfield at Stapleford Tawney; both are just to the north-east of London. Geographically, the sector also included No. 11 Group's forward operating airfield at Martlesham Heath, to the east of Ipswich, although this was mainly used by squadrons based at Debden during the Battle of Britain. Within the sector there was a line of radar sites covering the eastern approach to London and the south-east coast of East Anglia. The sites were at Canewdon, Walton, Bromley, Bawdsey and High Street. There was also a large anti-aircraft battery near Harwich and an Observer Corps centre near Colchester.

North Weald

Located about 3 miles to the south-east of Harlow in Essex, the airfield of North Weald was developed on land to the west of North Weald Bassett during the First World War. The first unit to take up residence, at the end of 1916, was a detachment of B.E.2cs of No. 39 Squadron. At that time the squadron was a home defence unit and regularly carried out night patrols, protecting London against Zeppelin raids and later Gotha bombers. After the war, No. 39 Squadron moved out and the base remained vacant for several years until it was developed as a fighter airfield in the late 1920s. This development included new hangars, improved accommodation and other facilities. The first squadron to occupy the new airfield was No. 56, in October 1927, with Siskins. The following year, Siskins of No. 29 Squadron arrived and North Weald remained home to both squadrons for several years. As part of the RAF's expansion programme during the mid-1930s, North Weald became home to Gloster Gauntlets of No. 151 Squadron in 1936 and Hawker Demons of No. 604 Squadron in 1938.

As the sector station for Sector E, North Weald was transformed into one of the most advanced airfields in Fighter Command. Its 400

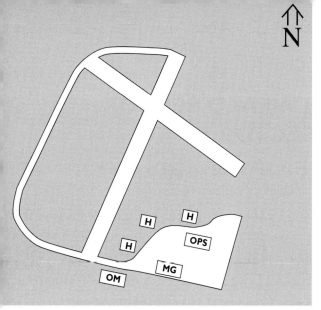

KEY:-

H = Hangars
OPS = Operations Block
OM = Officers' Mess
MG = Main Gate

acres of land was developed and the northern boundary was extended initially to facilitate four grass runways. Improvements during the final build-up to war included the development of two hard runways (one lying north-south and the other east-west) 900 yards in length, and an asphalt perimeter track was completed on the western side to ease movement around the airfield. Aircraft were accommodated in two A-type hangars and four blister hangars, with an additional four 'extra over blister' hangars. Airfield lighting and flares made operations at night possible and there were large storage facilities for fuel.

North Weald had the use of the satellite airfield at Stapleford Tawney and a decoy airfield at Nazeing. Although work commenced in October 1940 on another airfield at Hunsdon, which later became a second satellite for North Weald, it was not completed in time for use during the Battle of Britain.

When the battle opened there were two squadrons of Hurricanes, Nos 56 and 151, at North Weald. Both were involved in the early operations protecting shipping and convoys in the Channel. It was quite normal for one flight of Hurricanes to deploy forward to Manston and operate from there during the day. On the opening day of the battle, No. 56 Squadron deployed to Manston and was involved in action over the Channel, during which Flight Lieutenant 'Jumbo' Gracie destroyed a Bf110 between Ramsgate and Dover. His Hurricane was hit during the engagement but he managed to crash land successfully at Manston and was unhurt. It was his first kill; he went on to be credited with five enemy aircraft destroyed whilst serving with No. 56 Squadron at North Weald and was awarded the DFC.

No. 56 Squadron moved in to North Weald in June 1940 and were involved during the early days of the Battle of Britain. In the middle is Flight Lieutenant John Coghlan, OC 'A' Flight, who was awarded the DFC in July 1940 for six victories during the Battle of France. Coghlan left the squadron in early August but was killed just ten days later. Sitting in the entrance to the tent is Flying Officer Richard Brooker who was credited with two kills whilst serving with the squadron at North Weald. He was later awarded a DSO and DFC and bar but was killed just two weeks before the end of the war. The third pilot (standing left) is Pilot Officer Dryden.

Another squadron pilot to enjoy success on the opening day of the battle was Flight Sergeant Clifford Whitehead, who also destroyed a Bf110 in the area between Ramsgate and Dover. Whitehead had been one of the squadron's most successful sergeant pilots during the Battle of France, having destroyed three aircraft in two days during May. He later brought his total to five whilst at North Weald and was awarded the DFM. However, neither he nor Gracie survived the war; Gracie was killed in 1944 and Whitehead in 1942.

The first casualty from North Weald during the battle was Flying Officer James Allen of No. 151 Squadron, who went missing whilst the squadron was protecting the convoy 'Booty' during the morning of 12 July. He had engaged a formation of Do17s of KG2 east of Orfordness when he was caught in crossfire and was last seen descending into the Channel. His body was never recovered and he is remembered on the Runnymede Memorial.

One of the Do17s destroyed during the action of 12 July was shot down by North Weald's station commander, Wing Commander Victor Beamish, who flew with the squadrons at every opportunity throughout the Battle of Britain and became a legend at North Weald. Born in County Cork in 1903, he joined the RAF in 1925 and commanded Nos 64 and 504 Squadrons before taking command of North Weald in June 1940. During the Battle of Britain he was credited with three kills and claimed a further eight as 'probable'. He was awarded both a DSO and a DFC for his leadership in combat. Later, as a group captain, Beamish was awarded a bar to his DSO in

Flight Lieutenant 'Jumbo' Gracie was OC 'B' Flight, No. 56 Squadron and was credited with five kills whilst at North Weald during the Battle of Britain. He was awarded the DFC and later commanded a number of squadrons but was killed over Germany in February 1944.

September 1941 and was eventually credited with ten kills. However, whilst leading the North Weald Wing in March 1942, he was shot down by Bf109s over France and his aircraft was last seen entering cloud. He is also commemorated on the Runnymede Memorial.

No. 56 Squadron suffered its first losses during the afternoon of 13 July when Sergeants Joseph Whitfield and James Cowsill failed to return from a patrol between Dover and Calais. The squadron intercepted a large formation of aircraft bombing a convoy in the Channel but was engaged by the escorting Bf109s of JG51. They are both remembered on the Runnymede Memorial.

Both North Weald squadrons were involved throughout July and there were several losses. One in particular was Pilot Officer Jack Hamar of No. 151 Squadron who was killed at North Weald on 24 July. Having been told just the day before that he was to be awarded the DFC for the destruction of six enemy aircraft, Hamar crashed inverted on the airfield whilst attempting a roll prior to

Pictured whilst on stand-by at North Weald during the Battle of Britain is Flying Officer Bryan Wicks of No. 56 Squadron. Wicks was shot down in May over France and arrested as a spy. After his identity was eventually confirmed he returned to England and re-joined the squadron at North Weald in August 1940. Bryan Wicks was killed in Malta in October 1942 whilst commanding No. 126 Squadron. He was just twenty-two years old.

landing. During early August the North Weald squadrons became increasingly more involved as the air battle moved northwards from the Channel. This is evident from the increasing number of operational sorties flown by the two squadrons; from a combined total of about twenty sorties each day at the beginning of August to more than sixty a day from mid-August.

North Weald became one of the *Luftwaffe's* priority targets as every effort was made to destroy the airfields of Fighter Command. The opening day of the new campaign was 24 August and North Weald was subject to a heavy attack when some 200 bombs fell on it or in its immediate vicinity. Many of the station personnel fled for cover, using nearby Epping Forest as a natural shelter, and most of the damage was in the domestic and accommodation areas. Nine men from the Essex Regiment were killed when their shelter received a direct hit, and several more were injured. The attack also caused damage to the gas and water mains, and unexploded bombs around the airfield caused problems for several hours.

During the early morning of 31 August, it was the same again. A large force of more than 200 bombers were detected heading in from the south-east. The force split and one formation headed straight for North Weald. The Hurricanes of No. 56 Squadron were scrambled and they intercepted the raiders over Colchester but were bounced by the escorting Bf109s. The squadron did manage to break up much of the enemy formation but several Do17s got through to attack the airfield. However no significant damage was caused. No. 56 Squadron paid a price for its defence of its home base: four Hurricanes were shot down with the loss of one of the squadron's flight commanders, Flight Lieutenant Percy Weaver. His Hurricane crashed into the River Blackwater at West Point but his body was never recovered. At the time of his death he had destroyed seven aircraft during the battle. He is remembered on the Runnymede Memorial.

These latest losses made a total of eleven Hurricanes lost in just five days. The following day, the squadron moved to Boscombe Down to recover its strength. It was replaced at North Weald by No. 249 Squadron, no strangers to combat having already been involved in much of the action whilst operating from Boscombe Down with No. 10 Group. Indeed, Fighter Command's only VC of the war had been won on 16 August by one of its pilots, Flight Lieutenant James Nicolson. No. 151 Squadron also left North Weald for a rest and the Blenheims of No. 25 Squadron moved in.

The Hurricanes of No. 249 Squadron were immediately in action as the *Luftwaffe* increased its assault against Fighter Command's airfields.

During the morning of 3 September, North Weald was attacked once more. A force of thirty Do17s, escorted by Bf110s, was detected at 20,000 ft off the south-east coast and was tracked as it made its way up the Thames estuary towards the airfield. No. 249 Squadron had only just landed from a previous patrol and its Hurricanes were being refuelled when it was scrambled once more. Unfortunately, it did not have sufficient time to gain much height and could not prevent the attack. The Dorniers attacked from 15,000 ft and the airfield suffered severe damage. The hangars were hit and gutted by fire, and much damage was caused to the airfield and other buildings. The old operations block was virtually destroyed but the new block survived despite receiving a direct hit. More than 200 bombs fell on or around North Weald, most in the south and south-west part of the airfield. One Blenheim was destroyed on the ground, two station personnel were killed, seven were seriously injured and several more suffered slight injuries during the attack. However, despite being heavily cratered, the airfield remained open.

These latest attacks forced the dispersal of several facilities in order to keep North Weald open as an operational airfield and on 5 September the station's personnel were dispersed to different sites. The operations room was moved to a temporary location at Marden Ash, the station headquarters was set up at nearby Blake Hall, the sick quarters went to Bury Lodge in Bury Lane, and the MT vehicles were moved to Potter Street in Harlow.

The change in German tactics during September meant a welcome break from attacks on the airfield but there was to be no rest for No. 249 Squadron. During the late afternoon of 7 September the squadron lost four Hurricanes during an engagement with Bf109s over Maidstone. Two others had to crash land, one in Harlow and one at Eastchurch. One pilot was killed and three more wounded. One notable success was a first kill for Pilot Officer 'Ginger' Neil; a Bf109 over Ashford. This was the first of Neil's eleven kills whilst serving at North Weald, which brought him a DFC and bar at just twenty years old.

No. 249 Squadron had been reduced to seven serviceable Hurricanes by mid-September but the remaining pilots kept up the struggle. One other successful pilot during this period was one of the flight commanders, Flight Lieutenant 'Butch' Barton. He claimed four He111s on 11 September and two Do17s four days later. Whilst at North Weald during the battle, Barton brought his total to six confirmed kills, and he was awarded the DFC in October. Another successful pilot was Flying Officer George Barclay. His first success of the battle was a Bf109 south of Maidstone on 7 September and he destroyed a further three enemy aircraft during the battle whilst at the Weald.

There was also the occasional success at night for the Blenheims of No. 25 Squadron. Pilot Officer Michael Herrick, with Sergeant John Pugh, destroyed an He111 and a Do17 during the night of 4/5 September and another He111 on the night of 13/14 September. Michael Herrick was one of the RAF's first successful night-fighter pilots and was awarded the DFC at the end of the month.

A lone bomber dropped two bombs on North Weald during the early hours of 17 September; one landed on the western perimeter and the other landed in a nearby field. However, it was generally considered safe enough for the station to receive visitors. During early October there were visits from Sir Hugh Dowding and then from the Under Secretary of State, Captain Balfour.

The Blenheims of No. 25 Squadron moved out on 8 October and were replaced by the Hurricanes of No. 257 Squadron under the command of Squadron Leader Bob Tuck. By the time Tuck arrived at North Weald he had already destroyed fourteen enemy aircraft and had been awarded the DFC. During his short time there, he added two more Bf109s to his total and he was awarded a bar to his DFC later in the month. He went on to be one of the RAF's highest-scoring aces with twenty-seven confirmed kills, and he was also awarded a DSO and a second bar to his DFC.

North Weald suffered further attacks during October before the

Pilots of No. 249 Squadron with 'pipes various' during the Battle of Britain. From left to right is Pilot Officer George Barclay, Pilot Officer Percy Burton, Flying Officer Pat Wells and Pilot Officer Bryan Meaker. Tragically, both Percy Burton and Bryan Meaker were killed on 27 September whilst operating from North Weald. Only Pat Wells would survive the war as George Barclay was killed in North Africa in July 1942.

battle was officially over. A lone Dornier attacked on 27 October when it managed to drop below a large amount of cloud. Only one bomb hit the airfield; the rest landed in the local vicinity of Weald Gullet. Two days later the airfield was strafed and bombed by Bf109s of LG2. This attack proved quite successful, and one of the squadron's Hurricanes was destroyed whilst taking off and the pilot, Sergeant 'Jock' Girdwood, was killed, and dozens of bombs landed on the airfield, mostly on the operating areas but many also on the domestic site. Nineteen personnel were killed and more than forty were injured. Despite the extensive damage, however, North Weald remained open.

In the period immediately after the Battle of Britain, North Weald remained a front-line airfield within Fighter Command. No. 249 Squadron moved to Martlesham Heath on 7 November; just the start of several movements as offensive operations across the Channel increased. The airfield was also home to one of the American 'Eagle' Squadrons, No. 71, in 1941 and the Norwegians of Nos 331 and 332 Squadrons during the summer of 1942. Many fighter squadrons served at North Weald towards the end of the war, after which it was transferred to Transport Command and soon lost its flying units.

The airfield reverted to Fighter Command in 1949 and was modified to take the RAF's new jet fighters. It played its part in the post-war jet-fighter era during the early 1950s but was placed on care and maintenance in 1958. The RAF moved out altogether in 1964 and the site was transferred to the Army in 1966, although it remained open for light aircraft. Somewhat appropriately, in 1969, it was used during the making of the film *The Battle of Britain*.

During the 1970s a number of air shows took place from North Weald, including the first International Air Tattoo in 1971, and the airfield then became host to the world famous Fighter Meet from the mid-1980s. It continues to be home to a wide range of different aircraft with several original buildings still in existence. The former wartime airfield is also host to a wide range of local activities and can be clearly

One of the most successful fighter pilots of the war was Squadron Leader Bob Tuck who commanded No. 257 Squadron at North Weald during the Battle of Britain. He was eventually credited with twenty-seven kills for which he was awarded the DSO and DFC and two bars.

seen from the M11 when heading south just after Junction 7.

The memory of its former days lives on with the North Weald Airfield Museum, which is located in the former station office adjacent to what was the main entrance to the airfield. The address of the museum is: Ad Astra House, 6 Hurricane Way, North Weald, Essex, CM16 6AA, and it can be found to the north-east of Epping on the B181 Epping to Ongar road. Access is via the village of North Weald and not via the entrance to the current airfield. The museum is open every weekend from Easter to October and the opening hours are 12.00 noon to 5.00 p.m. Admission is £1.50 for adults and £1 for seniors and children under sixteen years old. The museum is a charitable trust and is dependent on income from entry, membership and donations. More details about it and the history of North Weald can be obtained on 01992 564200. In 2000 a permanent memorial located next to the museum was dedicated to those who served at RAF North Weald. Thirty-nine aircrew from the site and its satellite at Stapleford Tawney

Pilots of No. 249 Sqn at North Weald soon after the Battle of Britain. Standing third from the left is Pilot Officer 'Ginger' Neil who was credited with nine kills whilst at North Weald during the battle for which he was awarded the DFC and bar. Other pilots of note are Flying Officer John Beazley (second from left), Squadron Leader 'Butch' Barton (fourth from left) and Flying Officer Pat Wells (second from right). The mascot is 'Pipsqueak' and is sat with Pilot Officer Munro.

were killed during the Battle of Britain.

In addition to the Airfield Museum, there are a number of enthusiasts at North Weald keen to preserve the history of this famous airfield. One such organization is the North Weald Flying Service, a business operating out of the old airfield buildings which also has a membership and is actively involved in preserving the history of North Weald. Visitors are welcome to the club called The Squadron. Further details on membership or how to visit The Squadron can be obtained from Alan Couchman on 01992 524510. Access to The Squadron is via the main entrance to the airfield, which is on Merlin Way. It can be found by taking the A414 from the M11 towards Chelmsford. At the first roundabout turn right and then right at the next roundabout into Merlin Way and this leads to the main airfield entrance.

Sqn	From	To	Aircraft	Sqn Code
56 Sqn	Start (4/6/40)	1/9/40	Hurricane	LR/US
151 Sqn	Start (20/5/40)	29/8/40	Hurricane	DZ
249 Sqn	1/9/40	End (1/5/41)	Hurricane	GN
25 Sqn	1/9/40	8/10/40	Blenheim	ZK
257 Sqn	8/10/40	End (7/11/40)	Hurricane	DT

Summary of Squadrons at North Weald

The former main entrance to North Weald is now the site of the Airfield Museum and the permanent memorial dedicated to those who served at the airfield.

Stapleford Tawney

Located to the north-east of London, between Chigwell and Ongar, Stapleford Tawney, first opened in June 1934, when Edward Hillman required an airfield for his airline Hillman Airways. The land near the village of Stapleford Tawney was soon developed to include three small hangars and a passenger terminal. The airfield remained grass, but it did have concrete aircraft-operating areas in front of the hangars. The first aircraft to operate from the airfield were de Havilland Rapides. The company soon moved to Gatwick, and the airfield remained empty until the RAF expansion scheme, when it was used as a flying training school.

At the outbreak of the Second World War it was transferred to No. 11 Group as a satellite airfield for North Weald. There were four grass runways; the longest just over 1,200 yards, running from south-west to north-east, the second 1,100 yards from south-east to north-west, and the other two (north-south and east-west) 1,000 and 800 yards respectively. The airfield sloped towards the hangars in the northern part and there were several ridges running across the area, which was quite noticeable during take-off and landing. The improvements included a concrete perimeter track plus six dispersal sites, with new accommodation and administrative buildings.

When Stapleford Tawney reopened in March 1940 it was only capable of operating one squadron at a time, and it was used initially by the Hurricanes of either No. 56 or No. 151 Squadron based at nearby North Weald. Facilities were basic to say the least; home for the squadron's personnel and equipment were canvas marquee and bell tents plus a few corrugated iron huts.

The first squadron to be based at Stapleford was No. 151, which moved its Hurricanes in from North Weald on 29 August. This was during the height of the *Luftwaffe*'s attacks against Fighter Command's airfields, when North Weald became a priority target. Despite its close proximity to North Weald, Stapleford Tawney escaped any attack. However, No. 151 Squadron remained at Stapleford for just two days before moving north for a rest and being replaced by No. 46 Squadron, which remained at Stapleford until the end of the battle.

This squadron soon became involved in the action during the height of the battle in September. It suffered its first casualty from Stapleford on 2 September when Pilot Officer John Bailey was shot down over the Thames estuary. He had joined the squadron just days before and was twenty-two years old. The following day, No. 46 Squadron lost three Hurricanes during an attack on Ju88s, escorted by Bf109s, over

Rochford. One crashed at Redwood Creek in the River Crouch. The pilot, Sergeant Gerald Edworthy, was never found, and he is remembered on the Runnymede Memorial. Two more Hurricanes were lost on the following day during combat with Bf109s over Rochford; one pilot later died from his wounds.

Four days later, on 8 September, the squadron lost two more aircraft during combat over the Isle of Sheppey, and Sub-Lieutenant Jack Carpenter was killed. The young Fleet Air Arm pilot had already claimed a Bf110 and Bf109 in the previous few days of fighting but fell dead on this occasion despite having managed to bale out. He was just twenty-one years old and was buried at sea the following week.

Three days later the squadron was heavily involved in the fighting over the Thames estuary during the afternoon of 11 September. Three more Hurricanes were shot down with the loss of Sergeant William Peacock. At just twenty years old, Peacock was the squadron's fifth pilot killed in less than two weeks since the squadron had joined the battle at Stapleford, with several more wounded or injured.

Despite the losses, there were also successes for the squadron. One of the flight commanders, Flight Lieutenant Alex Rabagliati destroyed a Bf109 on 5 September, his second kill of the battle. During his time at Stapleford, Rabagliati destroyed a further five enemy aircraft and was awarded the DFC. Another successful pilot was Flying Officer 'Pip' Lefevre, who had been with the squadron since before the war. He destroyed a Ju88 near Southend on 3 September and then claimed a Do17 over the Isle of Sheppey on 8 September.

During the night of 7 October two bombs and a number of incendiaries fell on Stapleford Tawney. Apart from a few craters, there was no significant damage. Stapleford had also been home to Lysanders of No. 419 Flight, which had the task of dropping agents and supplies into occupied France, but the flight moved out to Stradishall on 9 October.

Operations continued from the airfield after the Battle of Britain as the RAF went on the offensive across the Channel. However, being grass meant that operations were impossible during the winter periods, when any large amount of rain meant that the ground became very boggy. Facilities were improved during the next couple of years and the station was transferred to No. 12 Group in 1943.

At the end of the war it was placed on care and maintenance. The land then mainly reverted to agriculture but was renovated during the 1950s and used by Herts and Essex Aero Club. It is now called Stapleford Airfield and is used by the Stapleford Flying Club.

The site can be found on the A113 towards Chigwell, on the southern side of the M25 and immediately on the left after passing the B175 turn-off to Romford. A propeller memorial stands outside the Stapleford Flying Club 'to those who gave their lives whilst serving at the airfield 1939–45'.

Sqn	From	To	Aircraft	Sqn Code
151 Sqn	29/8/40	1/9/40	Hurricane	DZ
46 Sqn	1/9/40	End (8/11/40)	Hurricane	PO

Summary of Squadrons at Stapleford Tawney

Martlesham Heath

Although geographically located in the North Weald Sector, Martlesham Heath was mainly used as a forward operating airfield for the Debden squadrons during the Battle of Britain. Located about 3 miles to the east of Ipswich in Suffolk, it was developed as the home of the Aeroplane Experimental Unit and first opened in early 1917. During the latter period of the First World War it was responsible for the testing and evaluation of aircraft belonging to the Royal Flying Corps as well as German aircraft that had been captured across the Channel.

At the end of the war the airfield was retained and in 1924 became the Aeroplance and Armament Experimental Establishment (A&AEE). It was famous as an experimental establishment during the inter-war years and was home to many different types of aircraft. During the period leading up to the Second World War it was involved in the testing of many of the RAF's newest types of aircraft including, crucially, the Hurricane and the Spitfire. As soon as the Second World War began the A&AEE moved out to Boscombe Down, which was

Stapleford Airfield is now the home of the Stapleford Flying Club.

considered to be a safer location to carry out its highly secretive work.

Its departure meant that the airfield was available as a forward operating airfield for No. 11 Group. No. 264 Squadron was the first resident unit at Martlesham but the Defiants moved out in the spring of 1940 and made way for the Blenheims of No. 25 Squadron, which operated in a night-fighter role. It was the only resident unit at Martlesham when the Battle of Britain began.

A few bombs fell in the vicinity of the airfield during the early hours of the opening day of the battle. Two days later No. 17 Squadron deployed there from its home base at Debden and operated throughout the day over the Channel. One successful pilot that day was Flying Officer Count Manfred Czernin, the son of an Austrian diplomat, who destroyed a Do17 of KG2 about 10 miles off Orfordness along the east coast of Suffolk. It was his sixth kill of the war and he was later credited with thirteen confirmed kills, plus five more shared, before he joined the SOE in 1943 and served as an agent in Italy operating behind enemy lines.

Various fighter squadrons used Martlesham during July and August but the most frequent visitors were the Hurricances of Nos 56 and 151 Squadrons from North Weald and Nos 17, 85, 111 and 257 from Debden. As there was no domestic and administrative accommodation, personnel had to spread out into the local area. Kesgrave Hall, for example, was used to accommodate some of the WAAF personnel.

The *Luftwaffe* attacked Martlesham Heath during the afternoon of 15 August. Bf110s and Bf109s of *Erprobungsgruppe* 210 carried out the attack from low level and caused considerable damage to the airfield and buildings, including two hangars that were totally destroyed. Fortunately, there were only a handful of casualties and none was fatal. There was a further attack on 20 August but this resulted in little damage.

On the night of 4/5 September a Blenheim of No. 25 Squadron claimed two He111s destroyed over the sea. The Blenheims moved out of Martlesham the following day and the Hurricanes of No. 257 Squadron moved in. Changes in the *Luftwaffe*'s tactics meant that Martlesham's position well to the north-east of London took it out of the front line of operations and its squadrons took an increasingly supportive role. No. 17 Squadron replaced No. 257 on 8 October and remained until the end of the battle.

There were two more attacks before the end of the battle. The first was by a lone bomber on 26 October and on the following day there was a further attack by about twenty Bf109s, but neither caused any significant damage.

Several different fighter squadrons operated from Martlesham after the Battle of Britain as the number of offensive operations across the Channel increased. The airfield was also used for a variety of purposes throughout the rest of the war; fighters were based there while taking part in gunnery and weapons practice over the sea, and it was an emergency airfield for crippled bombers returning from operations over Germany. The USAAF were also regular users, and Martlesham became home to the 356th Fighter Group from 1943 until the end of the war. It was also home to various aircraft of No. 277 Squadron, which carried out air-sea rescue duties from the airfield from December 1941 until April 1944.

After the war Martlesham was once again used as an experimental establishment and all the RAF's new jet aircraft passed through at some time or another. In 1955 the Whirlwind helicopters of No. 22 Squadron arrived at the airfield to carry out search and rescue duties. The airfield was also home to the Battle of Britain Memorial Flight from 1958 until 1961.

Flying activity from Martlesham was reduced during the early 1960s as the RAF gradually departed, and the airfield ceased flying operations in 1963. The site was then used for a while for light aircraft flying, then by the Post Office from the 1970s, and as home to the Suffolk Police headquarters. A small section of runway and taxiway remains but there is no longer any flying. Some of the old hangars and airfield buildings remain, although the site has now been developed for commercial and industrial purposes as well as housing.

The site can be found by taking the A14 from Ipswich towards Felixstowe and then taking the A12 northwards. After 3 miles the A12 passes through the site; the south-eastern area is dominated by BT's Adastral Park, which is clearly visible on approaching Martlesham Heath.

The history of the airfield lives on with the Martlesham Heath Aviation Society, which meets once a month, and the Control Tower Museum, which is based in the original control tower used throughout most of the Second World War. Admission to the museum is free but donations are most welcome. It is open every Sunday from Easter until the end of October and the opening hours are from 2.00 p.m. until 4.30 p.m. (other times are available through prior appointment). Details about the society and the museum are available on 01473 624510 or 01473 435104. Refreshments are available. Access to the museum is by a stairway, which means that there are unfortunately no facilities for the disabled. It is on the western side of the former airfield and can be found by remaining on the A12 until the Tesco Superstore roundabout, and then turning left into Eagle Way. Follow this round and turn right into Parkers Place and then left into The Grove. The museum is signposted and parking is available. Behind the museum it is possible to walk through a wooded area, which was part of the aircraft dispersal site.

There is also much to see around the site. By going back to the A12 roundabout and crossing the roundabout with Tesco on your left, you will come to Gloster Road on the right. Following this road back towards BT's Adastral Park you pass one of the original hangars on the right and other airfield buildings on the left before coming to Barrack Square, where there are some of the former buildings and two memorials opposite the BT site. One is to the USAAF and the other is to the RAF, the Dominions and Exiled Air Forces 'who gave their lives whilst operating from Martlesham Heath'. It was erected in 1990 during the 50th anniversary of the Battle of Britain.

Sqn	From	To	Aircraft	Sqn Code
25 Sqn	Start (19/6/40)	1/9/40	Blenheim	ZK
257 Sqn	5/9/40	8/10/40	Hurricane	DT
17 Sqn	8/10/40	End (28/2/41)	Hurricane	YB

Summary of Squadrons at Martlesham Heath

Left: The Control Tower Museum at Martlesham Heath.

The former dispersal site on the western side of the airfield (the Kesgrave side) can still be found in the wooded area behind the Control Tower Museum.

One of the large original hangars at Martlesham Heath is still standing and can be found in Gloster Road on the eastern side of the A12.

The two memorials at Martlesham Heath overlooking Barrack Square surrounded by some of the original buildings. On the left can be seen BT's Adastral Park, which dominates the south-eastern area of the former airfield.

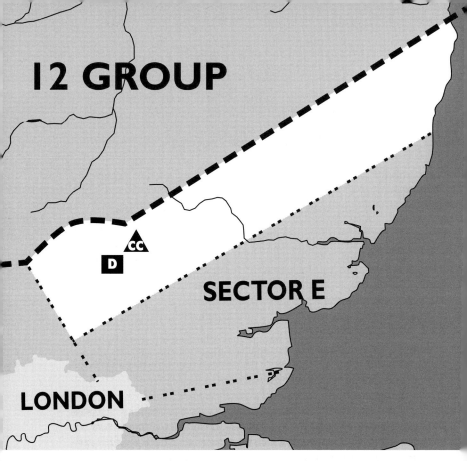

12 GROUP

SECTOR E

LONDON

SECTOR F – AUGUST 1940

KEY:-

D = Debden, Sector Airfield

CC = Castle Camps, Satellite Airfield

CHAPTER EIGHT

DEBDEN SECTOR
SECTOR F

The Debden Sector, or Sector F, was the furthest north of No. 11 Group's sector's and bordered No. 12 Group. There were two main airfields within it; the sector airfield of Debden itself and its satellite airfield at Castle Camps. Debden also used Martlesham Heath as a forward operating airfield during the Battle of Britain. Debden aircraft also used Wattisham on occasions but this airfield is not included in detail as it was not used operationally by No. 11 Group during the Battle of Britain. Also within the sector was the radar site at Dunwich.

Debden

Located just to the south-east of Saffron Walden in Essex, Debden airfield was developed as part of the RAF's expansion scheme during the mid-1930s as Britain prepared for the possibility of war. It opened in 1937 and was soon established as one of No. 11 Group's sector airfields with the capacity to accommodate up to three fighter squadrons at any one time. The airfield was grass with four runways. The longest was north-south (1,600 yards) and the other three (east-west, south-east–north-west and north-west–south-east) were all about 1,200 yards. Work carried out during the build up to the Second World War included the construction of three C-type hangars, technical, domestic and administration buildings and airfield defences.

The first squadrons to be based at Debden were Nos 73, 80 and 87, all equipped with Gladiators. As at most other fighter airfields, there were changes during the final months before the war. When war broke out Debden was home to Nos 85 and 87 Squadrons, which had by then both equipped with Hurricanes, and No. 29 Squadron equipped with Blenheims. Both Hurricane squadrons were immediately ordered to France and Debden then became home to the Hurricanes of Nos 17 and 504 Squadrons.

During the opening months of the Second World War fighters from Debden often deployed to its forward operating airfield at Martlesham Heath on the Suffolk coast, where patrols were flown. Meanwhile, further construction work had been carried out at Debden, which included further work on extending the runways and the addition of

147

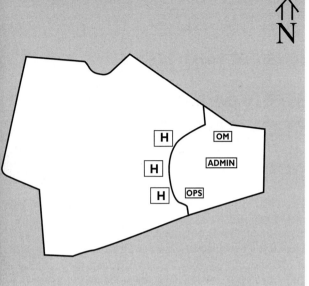

DEBDEN – 1940

KEY:-

H	= Hangars
OPS	= Operations Block
OM	= Officers' Mess
ADMIN	= Administration and Domestic Site

taxiways to ease the dispersal of its fighters. There was also work at nearby Castle Camps to develop it as a satellite airfield for Debden.

When the Germans attacked France and the Low Countries on 10 May, No. 504 Squadron moved across the Channel to join the air war over France and did not return to Debden. No. 85 Squadron returned to Debden at the end of May, having been in France since the outbreak of war. Command of this Squadron was given to Squadron Leader Peter Townsend who went on to become one of the most famous fighter pilots to have flown from Debden during the Battle of Britain. The Blenheims of No. 29 Squadron moved out soon after, which left just the two Hurricane squadrons, Nos 17 and 85 Squadrons, when the battle began.

Somewhat unusually the first bombs fell in the Debden area during the early morning of 10 July, the opening day of the battle. The local air defences opened up on a lone Do17 just as dawn was breaking and it dropped a number of small bombs, which landed in the local vicinity but not on the airfield itself. This was very much an isolated incident for the opening phase of the battle; the first few weeks generally involved both Debden squadrons carrying out patrols.

The first casualty from Debden during the battle was Sergeant Leonard Jowitt of No. 85 Squadron, who was operating from Martlesham Heath when he was shot down during an attack on an He111 of KG53 during the morning of 12 July. His Hurricane crashed into the sea off Felixstowe, he is commemorated on the Runnymede Memorial. No. 17 Squadron's first loss during the battle was Pilot Officer Henry Britton, who was killed on 6 August when his Hurricane

Squadron Leader Peter Townsend and ground crew of No. 85 Squadron. Townsend commanded the squadron during the Battle of Britain and personally destroyed three enemy aircraft whilst leading the squadron from Debden during the heavy aerial fighting on 18 August.

crashed soon after take-off on a routine air test. His aircraft came down in Debden Park. He was just nineteen years old and is buried in All Saint's churchyard at Wimbish, near Saffron Walden.

The Hurricanes of No. 257 Squadron moved to Debden on 15 August and four days later Nos 111 and 601 Squadrons arrived to replace Nos 17 and 85 Squadrons, which both moved further south, to Tangmere and Croydon respectively. Sadly, No. 85 Squadron had lost one of its most experienced fighter pilots and one of its most popular characters just the day before when Flying Officer 'Dickie' Lee was reported missing. The godson of Lord Trenchard, he had joined the RAF in 1935 and was posted to No. 85 Squadron in 1938. Although details of his wartime successes in France are unclear, he is believed to have destroyed nine enemy aircraft for which he was awarded the DSO and DFC. On 18 August, he was one of thirteen Hurricanes from No. 85 Squadron that intercepted a large formation of about 200 He111s of KG53 and Ju88s, escorted by Bf110s of ZG26, 15 miles to the east of

Hurricanes of No. 85 Squadron. This squadron had served in France and then at Debden during the Battle of Britain. It moved briefly to Castle Camps during early September before being moved north for a well earned rest.

Foulness Island. He was last seen just before 6.00 p.m. chasing an enemy formation of either Ju88s or Bf110s out to sea about 30 miles off the coast. He was twenty-three years old and is commemorated on the Runnymede Memorial.

The number of operational sorties flown from Debden increased throughout August as its squadrons became increasingly involved in the air battle; they rose from about twenty per day at the beginning of the month to more than sixty a day by mid-August.

During the following week the *Luftwaffe* turned its attention to the airfields of Fighter Command and Do17s carried out an attack on Debden during the afternoon of 26 August, which resulted in some considerable damage. Many buildings received direct hits and five of the station's personnel were killed. The airfield was also left cratered and one Hurricane belonging to No. 257 Squadron was destroyed on the ground. There was a further attack during the early morning of 31 August, which caused further damage to the airfield and buildings. Two formations of Do17s from KG2, escorted by Bf110s, attacked from medium level. Debden's three squadrons were all airborne and patrolling at 15,000 ft, although two had been dispersed, with No. 111 operating from Castle Camps and No. 257 Squadron from Martlesham Heath. The Hurricanes intercepted the attackers at 16,000 ft and claimed nine enemy aircraft destroyed. Three Debden Hurricanes were shot down, one from No. 111 Squadron and two from No. 257 with the loss of one pilot killed. However,

The South African ace Pilot Officer Albert 'Day' Lewis served with No. 85 Squadron at Debden during the Battle of Britain. He was eventually credited with eighteen kills and was awarded the DFC and bar.

several bombs landed across the airfield and some buildings received direct hits. Two station personnel were killed and a dozen more were injured.

Although No. 601 Squadron escaped the morning encounter with just one Hurricane damaged, the squadron did lose four Hurricanes later in the day when Bf109s engaged it over the Thames estuary during the early afternoon; one pilot was missing. One pilot who escaped with his life during the engagement was Flying Officer Humphrey Gilbert, who was shot down by a Bf109 but managed to bale out. He had only been with the squadron for two weeks but had already been involved in the destruction of three aircraft. He was shot down for a second time the following week whilst operating from Tangmere but, once again, baled out. He later commanded a squadron at Debden before he was killed in May 1942 whilst attempting to take off from the airfield, apparently on his way to a party with one of the airfield's controllers on his lap. He is buried in Saffron Walden Cemetery.

Flying Officer Humphrey Gilbert served with No. 601 Squadron at Debden during the Battle of Britain. He later commanded No. 65 Squadron at Debden but was killed in May 1942 whilst attempting to take off from the airfield on the way to a party with one of the airfield's controllers on his lap.

Although Debden remained fully operational during the attacks, the operations room was moved to a temporary facility near Saffron Walden. There were further changes to the squadrons during the first week of September. No. 17 returned to Debden on 2 September, to replace No. 601 Squadron, and No. 85 Squadron returned to replace No. 111, which moved south to Croydon the following day. No. 85 Squadron moved immediately to Castle Camps but remained for just two days before it moved north for a rest. On 5 September, No. 73 Squadron replaced No. 257, which moved to Martlesham Heath; the new arrivals moved immediately to Castle Camps.

No. 17 Squadron remained at Debden and was involved in some of the heavy

The grave of Squadron Leader Humphrey Gilbert at Saffron Walden Cemetery, Essex.

action during September before it moved to Martlesham Heath on 8 October. No. 25 Squadron, equipped with Beaufighters and Blenheims, moved in to Debden in a night-fighter role to counter the increasing number of raids against London by night. The squadron's first operational night patrol was flown on 10 October and the Beaufighter scored its first victory on 15 November, just after the battle was officially over.

After the Battle of Britain Debden was home to various squadrons and the Debden Wing was formed in 1941; over the next year it carried out many successful fighter sweeps across the Channel. From 1943 Debden was home to three USAAF fighter squadrons, which were amongst the first to provide long range fighter escort for bombers of the US Eighth Air Force.

At the end of the war the Americans moved out and Debden was used for technical training until 1960 and then by the RAF Police until it closed in 1975. During this period it was used for the filming of *The Battle of Britain*. The site was then transferred to the Army and many of the airfield's hangars and buildings were demolished. It was renamed Carver Barracks and now is used by the Army for training.

It can be found by taking the B184 from Thaxted towards Saffron Walden. Just after Howlett End turn left and Carver Barracks is on the right. It is not possible to gain access to the site without prior permission but the small public roads can be followed past the southern edge of the airfield. The southern end of the north–south runway is clearly visible and by turning right you can pass the western boundary. Returning along the same route, keeping the former airfield and the barracks on the left, you pass the eastern side of the airfield on the B184 towards Saffron Walden.

Saffron Walden Cemetery. Buried in the front row (left) are *Oberleutnant* Heidereich and *Unteroffizer* Panczach of KG2 who were both killed when their Do17Z was shot down during the attack on Debden on 26 August.

The former airfield at Debden has been retained by the MoD and is now Carver Barracks. The Army uses the airfield for training and one of the main runways is visible from the road passing the southern end of the site.

Sqn	From	To	Aircraft	Sqn Code
17 Sqn	Start (19/6/40) 2/9/40	19/8/40 8/10/40	Hurricane Hurricane	YB
85 Sqn	Start (22/5/40) 3/9/40	19/8/40 5/9/40	Hurricane	VY
257 Sqn	15/8/40	5/9/40	Hurricane	DT
111 Sqn	19/8/40	3/9/40	Hurricane	TM
601 Sqn	19/8/40	2/9/40	Hurricane	UF
25 Sqn	8/10/40	End (27/11/40)	Blenheim Beaufighter	ZK

Summary of Squadrons at Debden

Castle Camps

The site of this former airfield is in a remote location on the East Anglian Heights about 10 miles to the north-east of Debden and about 3 miles to the south-west of Haverhill in Essex. It was first developed at the outbreak of the Second World War as a satellite for Debden. The facilities were very basic: there were no permanent buildings, which meant that the pilots and ground crew had to operate from, and sleep in, tented accommodation. The first unit to make use of the airfield was No. 85 Squadron, which arrived just as the Battle of Britain began. No. 111 Squadron also regularly deployed to Castle Camps during the last two weeks of August when it was based at Debden.

The first casualty at Castle Camps was Pilot Officer John Bickerdike of No. 85 Squadron, who crashed whilst attempting to land during the late afternoon of 22 July. He was from New Zealand and had travelled to England to join the RAF soon after the outbreak of the

153

Second World War. He joined the squadron at the end of May and claimed his first success on 12 July whilst attacking He111s and Do17s over the Channel. He is buried in Wimbish Parish Church cemetery, near Saffron Walden.

No. 85 Squadron moved in to Castle Camps on 3 September but remained for only two days before it moved north for a rest. With its departure, No. 73 Squadron moved in on 5 September as the first resident unit, having been moved south to Debden to join the battle. The squadron was in action immediately and intercepted He111s of KG53 over the Thames estuary; it lost four Hurricanes and one pilot in that first afternoon.

The squadron was also heavily involved in the action of 7 September when the *Luftwaffe* turned its attention to bombing London. It claimed at least three Bf110s destroyed but lost one of its more experienced pilots, Flight Lieutenant Reg Lovett, who was shot down in the late afternoon. He had been a flight commander with the squadron since the outbreak of war and was credited with three kills. He had been shot down over Burnham just two days before but managed on that occasion to bale out. His luck, however, ran out on 7 September when he was shot down and crashed near Billericay.

The squadron suffered on 14 September when it lost three Hurricanes destroyed and a further four damaged during an engagement over Kent and the Thames estuary; one pilot was killed. As the *Luftwaffe* started bombing more by night, No. 73 Squadron operated as a night-fighter unit to counter the raids against London, but without any success.

During late September and early October, No. 257 Squadron deployed to Castle Camps on a daily basis from its base at Martlesham Heath. Together with No. 73 Squadron from Castle Camps and No. 17 from Martlesham Heath, the three squadrons operated successfully during the final weeks of the battle.

After the battle No. 73 Squadron left for the Middle East and Castle Camps was temporarily unoccupied whilst further work was carried out, including construction of extended runways and permanent buildings. No. 157 Squadron reformed at Debden in December 1941 and immediately moved to Castle Camps. It received Mosquitos during early 1942 and was the RAF's first Mosquito night-fighter squadron. In March 1943 No. 605 Squadron, also equipped with Mosquitos, replaced No. 157 Squadron and soon after Castle Camps became a satellite of North Weald. In 1944 the airfield was also home to Blenheims, Spitfires, Typhoons and Tempests.

After the war, activity rapidly reduced and the airfield closed in 1946. The site was never used again for flying and the land has long since been recovered for farming. There are few reminders of the airfield, although remnants of buildings and the airfield's perimeter track remain, and there is a memorial commemorating the RAF airfield.

The site can be found by working either south from the A1307 Linton to Haverhill road or working north from the B1054 to the east of Saffron Walden. Either way, the roads are very narrow but the site of the former airfield is just to the south of the village of Castle Camps, on the road to Helions Bumpstead. The memorial is on the right just before leaving Castle Camps. Just a short distance beyond it is a small private track to the right, which marks the boundary between Cambridgeshire and Essex, This track provides a good reference point for what was the central area of the airfield.

Sqn	From	To	Aircraft	Sqn Code
85 Sqn	3/9/40	5/9/40	Hurricane	VY
73 Sqn	5/9/40	End (13/11/40)	Hurricane	TP

Summary of Squadrons at Castle Camps

The memorial to the former airfield in Castle Camps village.

The former airfield at Castle Camps has long reverted to agriculture. The private track passing through the site now marks the boundary between Cambridgeshire to the right and Essex to the left.

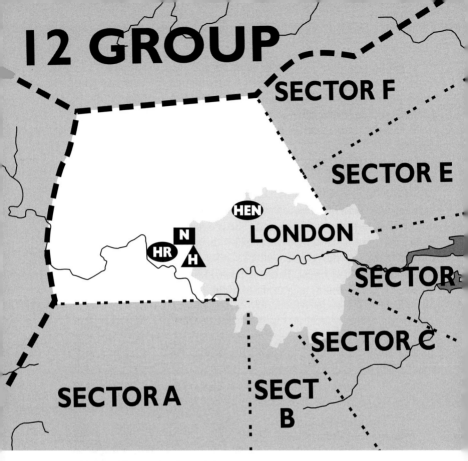

12 GROUP

SECTOR F

SECTOR E

HEN **LONDON**

N

HR

H

SECTOR ...

SECTOR C

SECTOR A

SECT B

SECTOR Z – AUGUST 1940

KEY:-

N = Northolt, Sector Airfield

H = Heston, Satellite Airfield

HEN = Hendon, Operating Airfield

HR = Heathrow, Operating Airfield

CHAPTER NINE

NORTHOLT SECTOR
SECTOR Z

The Northolt Sector, or Sector Z, covered the area to the west and north-west of London out as far as the boundary with No. 10 Group to the west and No. 12 Group to the north. It contained just one major airfield of No. 11 Group, the sector airfield of Northolt itself. Owing to its close proximity to London, Northolt was used extensively during the Battle of Britain, in particular during the defence of London itself.

The sector also included the airfields of Hendon, Heston and Heathrow, all of which were used at some time during the Battle of Britain. Hendon, in particular, was also used in the defence of the capital and there are few more famous incidents than that of Sergeant Ray Holmes of No. 504 Squadron, who shot down the bomber that bombed Buckingham Palace on 15 September 1940. Brief details of these three airfields are included for completeness. However, although Luton was used briefly by a detachment of Defiant night fighters from No. 264 Squadron at Kirton-in-Lindsey, this airfield has been excluded.

Of all the airfields included in this book, Northolt is the only one that remains in use by the RAF today. This is probably due to its proximity to London, but its legacy as a Battle of Britain airfield has lived on with the Polish Air Force Memorial, on the main A40 Western Avenue just outside the airfield boundary, which was erected just after the Second World War. For Hendon, too, the history of the RAF has lived on, as the site is now home of the RAF Museum.

Also within the Northolt Sector were HQ Fighter Command at Bentley Priory and HQ No. 11 Group at Uxbridge. There was also a heavy anti-aircraft battery at Langley, near Slough, and an Observer Corps centre near Watford. Finally, no visit to this sector would be complete without a visit to the Runnymede Memorial between Staines and Windsor, which commemorates those airmen who have no known graves; brief details of Runnymede are therefore also included.

Northolt

Northolt is located about 15 miles to the west of London, on the A40 Western Avenue. The land was first considered for use as an aerodrome in 1910, during the very first days of powered flight but for various reasons the plans came to nothing. It was not until 1915 that it opened, when sites were needed for home defence landing grounds for the Royal Flying Corps. The airfield was developed during 1915 and 1916 but poor drainage always made flying operations difficult during the winter months. It was essentially used as a training aerodrome throughout the First World War and a number of squadrons visited the site in preparation for operational service overseas. The US entry into the war during 1917 brought Americans there for training and there were soon three fully established training squadrons with over fifty aircraft and 100 students at any one time.

With the First World War over the training squadrons were disbanded and Northolt became a joint military/civil airfield in 1919, although it always maintained a reasonably strong military presence, as it was the nearest airfield to the RAF Depot at Uxbridge. During the early 1920s it was briefly home to DH9As of No. 12 Squadron but from 1923 it was the permanent home of No. 41 Squadron until 1935, during which time it operated Snipes, Siskins, Bulldogs and Demons. In the mid-1920s it was also briefly home to two of the RAF's new auxiliary squadrons. These moved out to Hendon in 1927 and were replaced by No. 24 Squadron, which operated a variety of aircraft and its responsibilities included flying senior members of the air staff to meetings and appointments from the Air Ministry. The unit remained until 1933 when it also moved to Hendon.

No. 111 Squadron, equipped with Bulldogs, arrived in July 1934 and remained until the outbreak of the Second World War, being joined in 1936 by the Demons of No. 23 Squadron. By the time that war was declared, Northolt had been officially transferred to No. 11 Group and the airfield was one of the first to have a C-type hangar built as its second permanent aircraft hangar. Also, two paved runways, 800 yards long, had been laid, which made Northolt one of the few airfields to have hardened runways by the outbreak of the war.

At the start of the Battle of Britain, Northolt was home to the Hurricanes of Nos 1 and 257 Squadrons. The first encounter during the battle was on 19 July when No. 257 Squadron shared in the destruction of a Do17 near Brighton and No. 1 Squadron engaged He111s of KG55. As part of several moves by squadrons of No. 11 Group during the early phase of the battle, No. 1 Squadron exchanged places with No. 43 Squadron at Tangmere for a week at the end of July before it returned to Northolt on 1 August.

No. 303 Squadron was formed at Northolt on 22 July and was made up of Polish personnel evacuated from France. The squadron received its first Hurricanes at the end of the month and commenced training flights in early August. Because of their lack of English-speaking pilots, the Poles were initially kept out of the front line. The station commander at the time was Group Captain Stanley Vincent, a fighter ace from the First World War who had remained in the post-war RAF. He had commanded Northolt previously in 1937 and had returned in March 1940. He was to become a legend at Northolt during the Battle of Britain; he always made sure that a Hurricane was made available to him whenever possible and, at forty-three, was one of the oldest men to fly in the battle. He went on to become AOC No. 11 Group after the war.

The first deaths of Northolt pilots during the battle occurred on 8 August when No. 257 Squadron encountered Bf109s of JG27 off St Catherine's Point; three pilots failed to return. Flight Lieutenant Noel Hall had been a flight commander with the squadron since May 1940 and is buried in France. Flying Officer Brian D'Arcy-Irvine and Sergeant Kenneth Smith are both remembered on the Runnymede Memorial. Three days later No. 1 Squadron lost its first pilot when Pilot Officer John Davey was shot down during combat with Bf110s over the Isle of Wight. He was killed whilst attempting a forced landing on Sandown golf course and is buried in Sandown Cemetery.

No. 257 Squadron was replaced at Northolt by No. 1 (RCAF) Squadron, which moved in from Croydon on 16 August. The Canadians were declared operational the following day, which meant that all three squadrons at Northolt were of different nationalities.

Much had been done to prepare the airfield and the squadrons for the expected onslaught from the *Luftwaffe*. Aircraft dispersal pens were constructed in various parts of the airfield and nearby Heston was used as a satellite airfield. Furthermore, much had been done to conceal Northolt from the air by the use of camouflage and efforts had been made to confuse the enemy by the construction of a dummy airfield on the golf course at Barnet. Whilst it is not clear how many attacks were ever planned against Northolt, all this effort seems to have proved successful as the airfield escaped any significant damage.

Because of its close proximity to London and its mix of nationalities, Northolt received a number of distinguished visitors during the battle. One was the Prime Minister, Winston Churchill, who called in occasionally on his way to his residence at Chequers.

Although No. 303 Squadron had been kept out of operations during August, the situation changed on 30 August following a training flight over Hertfordshire. A young Pole, Flying Officer Ludwig Paszkiewicz, spotted enemy bombers nearby. He transmitted his sighting but received no reply from his formation leader, Squadron Leader Ronald Kellett. The frustration of being kept out of the front line for so long suddenly got the better of him and he did not hesitate in attacking a Do17 bomber to give the squadron its first victory. Whilst some considered this as a lack of discipline in the air, Dowding immediately declared the Poles operational and they went on to fight with distinction throughout the remainder of the battle and, indeed, the war.

No. 1 Squadron moved north for a rest on 9 September and was replaced by No. 229 Squadron. All three Northolt squadrons were involved in the action over the south-east during the afternoon of 11 September, which resulted in seven Hurricanes failing to return. All the losses occurred during thirty minutes of fighting just after 4.00 p.m. During an attack against He111s over TunbridgeWells, No. 1(RCAF) Squadron and No. 229 Squadron each lost two aircraft; fortunately, all the pilots survived. However, No. 303 Squadron lost two pilots who were shot down by Bf109s over London. Sergeant Stefan Wojtowicz was killed when his Hurricane crashed at Westerham and he is buried in Northwood Cemetery in Middlesex. Flying Officer Arsen Cebrzynski crashed in Pembury and died from his injuries the following week. A third Hurricane from the squadron was damaged during the same combat but managed to force land at Heston.

All three squadrons were also involved during the action of 15 September. At midday No 1(RCAF) Squadron lost two Hurricanes, which were shot down by Bf109s over Tunbridge Wells; one pilot was killed. During the same air activity No. 229 Squadron also lost two aircraft and Belgian Pilot Officer Georges Doutrepont. His Hurricane crashed on Staplehurst Station. The Poles were also involved later in the afternoon when Bf109s engaged No. 303 Squadron over the Kent coast. Within the space of ten minutes, the Poles had seven Hurricanes either shot down or damaged. Five aircraft managed to return to Northolt but two were lost, as was Sergeant Michal Brzezowski, who is remembered on the Polish Air Force Memorial at Northolt.

Group Captain Stanley Vincent also took part in the fighting. Although he made claims during the day he was operating alone and the claims could not be verified. However, he was credited with two Bf109s two weeks later and became the only RAF pilot to have shot down enemy aircraft in both world wars; his previous kill had occurred in January 1917 over the Western Front.

A detachment of Defiants of No. 264 Squadron operated from

Northolt for a few days in mid-September. The first bombs fell on the airfield during the evening of 25 September. Dropped by a lone bomber, they landed in the north-east corner, but there was no significant damage and there were no casualties.

King George VI visited the station the following day, and during his visit two of the squadrons were scrambled to meet a large formation heading for the Supermarine factory at Woolston in Southampton. The King listened to the battle as it took place from the makeshift sector operations room in a shop in Ruislip. After the action he remained at Northolt to meet the pilots on landing.

A second attack on Northolt took place on 6 October when a lone Ju88 dropped two bombs and strafed buildings from low level on its way across the airfield. One airman was killed and one Hurricane of No. 303 Squadron was destroyed on the ground. The pilot, Sergeant Antoni Siudak was killed and is buried in Northwood Cemetery, Middlesex, as is the airman, AC2 Stennett.

Northolt suffered a tragic loss on 8 October when Sergeant Josef Frantisek of No. 303 Squadron was killed during a routine morning patrol. His Hurricane crashed in Ewell, Surrey, although the circumstances are unknown. Frantisek was a Czech pilot who had fought with the Polish and French air forces before making his way to England to continue his fight against the Germans. He had joined No. 303 Squadron when it formed at Northolt and destroyed seventeen enemy aircraft, which made him the top-scoring pilot during the Battle of Britain and brought him the award of the DFM. This was a remarkable achievement considering his first victory was on 2 September and his final one on 30 September. He is buried in Northwood Cemetery, Middlesex.

On 10 October the Canadians moved north for a rest and were replaced by No. 615 Squadron, which remained at Northolt for the remainder of the battle. The following day No. 303 Squadron also left Northolt and moved north for a rest and another Polish squadron, No. 302, replaced it. A combination of poor weather and the *Luftwaffe* changing to night bombing resulted in less activity from Northolt

The Czech ace Sergeant Josef Frantisek of No. 303 Squadron who was the highest scoring pilot in the Battle of Britain. Whilst at Northolt Frantisek destroyed seventeen aircraft during September 1940 but was killed on 8 October.

A Hurricane of No. 615 Squadron at Northolt during the last weeks of the battle.

during the latter days of the battle. There was, however, a tragic chain of events that led to the loss of four pilots from No. 302 Squadron on 18 October. Poor weather during the late afternoon led to a flight of Hurricanes becoming lost over Surrey. One crashed at Thames Ditton whilst attempting a forced landing, a second crashed at Boxley having run out of fuel and the other two crashed on the race course at Kempton Park. A fifth successfully made a forced landing. It was a tragic end to the squadron's first week in the operational theatre.

The last casualty from Northolt during the battle was another pilot of No. 302 Squadron, Flight Lieutenant Franciszek Jastrzebski, who failed to return from a patrol over the Channel on 25 October. He is remembered on the Polish Air Force Memorial at Northolt.

By mid-1941 all the squadrons based at Northolt were Polish and it generally stayed that way for the next few years. Nearby Heston was upgraded from a satellite airfield to full station status during 1942 and four Polish squadrons, two at each base, operated together as a Polish wing. In mid-1943 Northolt became Transport Command's main airfield in the London area, as its headquarters was at nearby Stanmore. In April 1944 the Polish squadrons all left and Northolt was increasingly used by transport aircraft for the remainder of the war.

Several improvements were made to Northolt during the latter stages of the war, including a runway extension and a new B1-type hangar. When the war was over, it was an ideal choice for London's main airport while Heathrow was being reconstructed, and it was officially loaned to the Ministry of Civil Aviation. Many European commercial airlines operated from there until it was handed back to the RAF in 1954.

Northolt has been used by transport aircraft ever since and the role of providing VIP transport remains one of its main roles. Today, it is still used by the RAF and is home to No. 32 Squadron, which operates a variery of aircraft including BAe 125s and 146s and Squirrel helicopters and incorporates the aircraft of the former Queen's Flight. Although the A40 Western Avenue passes along the southern part of the airfield there are no stopping points from which to observe the airfield or flying. Furthermore, as it is an active airfield, there is no public access unless by prior arrangement.

Northolt's connection with its wartime role is marked by the Polish Air Force Memorial, which is located just outside the airfield's south-eastern boundary and can be accessed from a slip road off the A40 Western Avenue. It is constructed of stone, surmounted by a bronze eagle, and was unveiled on 2 November 1948. On the back is inscribed 'I have fought a good fight, I have finished my course, I have kept the faith.' More than 1,200 Polish airmen are commemorated on the memorial, including twenty-nine killed in action during the Battle of Britain.

The entrance to RAF Northolt can be found by turning left off the A40 towards London at the Polish Air Force Memorial, towards Northwood. It is about 400 yards on the left.

Sqn	From	To	Aircraft	Sqn Code
257 Sqn	Start (4/7/40)	14/8/40	Hurricane	DT
1 Sqn	Start (18/6/40) 1/8/40	23/7/40 9/9/40	Hurricane	JX
43 Sqn	23/7/40	1/8/40	Hurricane	NQ
303 Sqn	22/7/40	11/10/40	Hurricane	RF
1 Sqn (RCAF)	16/8/40	10/10/40	Hurricane	YO
229 Sqn	9/9/40	End (15/12/40)	Hurricane	RE
615 Sqn	10/10/40	End (17/12/40)	Hurricane	KW
302 Sqn	11/10/40	End (23/11/40)	Hurricane	WX

Summary of Squadrons at Northolt

The entrance to RAF Northolt today. Of all the airfields used by No. 11 Group during the Battle of Britain, Northolt is the only one still in use by the RAF.

The Polish Air Force Memorial at Northolt.

Hendon

Situated just to the north of central London, between Edgware and Hendon, this famous airfield was home to many fighter squadrons during the Second World War but only one was based there during the Battle of Britain. No. 504 Squadron, which was equipped with Hurricanes spent three weeks at Hendon during September 1940. Hurricanes of Nos 1 and 303 Squadrons from nearby Northolt also used the airfield on occasions.

The origins of the airfield date back to 1909–10 when the site near Colindale was first used for test flying early aeroplanes. By the First World War it had been developed into an aerodrome and was used by various aircraft manufacturers in the local area, as well as being a venue for flying instruction and for early flying displays. It was then requisitioned as a station for the Royal Naval Air Service and was used for a number of purposes during the First World War, including aircraft manufacture, as an aircraft acceptance park, pilot training and the home defence of London.

After the First World War, it was retained as a military airfield but was also used for civil aviation. It was transferred to the RAF in 1925, and is probably best be remembered for hosting the annual charity RAF Displays (originally known as the RAF Tournaments) from 1920 until 1937. Indeed, the Spitfire and the Hurricane made their first public appearance at Hendon in 1936. During the inter-war years it was also home to various squadrons of the Auxiliary Air Force and it also hosted one of several Empire Air Days in 1939.

When the Second World War broke out Hendon was home to No. 24 Squadron, a communications squadron that had arrived at Hendon in 1933 and was to remain at the airfield throughout the Second World War. Hurricanes of No. 257 Squadron were based there for a few weeks from May 1940 but left by the time the Battle of Britain began. As already mentioned, No. 504 Squadron was the only operational squadron at Hendon during the Battle of Britain, having moved south on 5 September.

The squadron soon suffered its first loss when Flying Officer Ken Wendel from New Zealand died of his injuries after Bf109s shot him down whilst he was leading a section over the Thames estuary during the afternoon of 7 September. The squadron suffered a further loss just four days later when Pilot Officer Arthur Clarke went missing during combat over Kent on the afternoon of 11 September. His body was never found and he is commemorated on the Runnymede Memorial. Although the wreckage of his Hurricane was located near Newchurch,

Romney Marsh, it was decided that his remains should be undisturbed and a memorial was dedicated forty-six years later to the day, on 11 September 1986.

One of the most famous incidents of the Battle of Britain occurred on 15 September when a Hurricane flown by Sergeant Ray Holmes of No. 504 Squadron from Hendon shot down a Do17 over the centre of London. The Dornier was reported to have bombed Buckingham Palace and the wreckage fell on Victoria Station. Quite amazingly, it was the only German aircraft to come down in the centre of London during the Battle of Britain. Ray Holmes was hit by return fire and baled out; he landed in Chelsea and his Hurricane crashed in Buckingham Palace Road. Many people on the ground witnessed the action, and the incident came to the public's attention, once again, when parts of his Hurricane were excavated live on television during the build-up to the 60th anniversary of D-Day in 2004. Most appropriately Ray Holmes was the star of the show as he was present at the site to see parts of his Hurricane for the first time in sixty-four years.

Two other successful pilots on 15 September were Squadron Leader John Sample and Pilot Officer Michael Rook. Johnny Sample had commanded No. 504 Squadron since May 1940 and had already been awarded the DFC in June following the Battle of France. The Do17 he claimed on 15 September was his third kill of the war.

Although they were led by an experienced commanding officer, most of No. 504 Squadron's young pilots were in action for the first time whilst at Hendon. Michael Rook's claim of a Do17, also on 15 September, was his first of the war. He was one of two brothers serving with the squadron at the same time; his brother, Flight Lieutenant Tony Rook, was one of the flight commanders.

The squadron suffered just one further loss, Sergeant Denis Helcke, who was killed during a training flight on 17 September. The Squadron then moved out of Hendon on 26 September to its new base at Filton in Bristol.

Hendon was home to various units during the Second World War, most of which were involved with communications or air transport. By the end of the war they had moved out, which left just No. 24 Squadron still in residence, having been there throughout the war. The airfield's close proximity to London made it ideal for ferrying VIPs around. However, within a year of the war ending the squadron had moved out. The airfield was used briefly by the Auxiliary Air Force before flying ceased in 1949. The area around the airfield was developed for housing, which meant that it could not be expanded. It was therefore unsuitable for modern commercial and transport aircraft, and finally closed in 1957.

The legacy of the RAF lives on with the RAF Museum, which is situated on the former airfield and first opened in 1972. It is signposted from the A1 just south of the Mill Hill junction with the A41 (close to Junction 2 of the M1). The nearest London Underground station is Colindale on the Northern Line towards Edgware, and it is only a short walk to the museum.

The museum is open daily 10.00 am to 6.00 pm. (including Bank Holidays). Last admission is at 5.30 pm. The museum is closed 24-26 December and 1 January. Admission is free and the main attraction for the Battle of Britain enthusiast is the Battle of Britain Hall, which retells the story of this famous battle.

Sqn	From	To	Aircraft	Sqn Code
504 Sqn	5/9/40	26/9/40	Hurricane	TM

Summary of Hendon

Heston

Located about 15 miles to the west of London, just to the north of Hounslow, Heston was used by No. 11 Group as a satellite airfield for Northolt. Its origins date back to 1929; it was used for civil aviation during the 1930s. The RAF requisitioned it as a satellite airfield at the outbreak of the Second World War and it was used throughout the Battle of Britain by No. 1 Photographic Reconnaissance Unit (PRU). Commanded by Wing Commander Geoffrey Tuttle, the unit operated eleven high-altitude Spitfires and its role included locating invasion barges across the channel. It was very successful, and reported and photographed hundreds of barges during the week of 6–11 September during the German build-up to the planned invasion of England.

The airfield was considered important enough by the Germans to be included amongst its targets during September, when the *Luftwaffe* started bombing London. After the battle, Heston was upgraded from a satellite airfield to full station status during 1942, after which two Polish squadrons were based there with two Northolt squadrons operating as a Polish wing.

Heston remained an active airfield throughout the Second World War, after which the development of Heathrow nearby brought an end to aviation there and it closed in 1946. The site has long been

167

developed for housing and commercial business and the M4 now passes through the middle.

Heathrow

London's Heathrow Airport, about 20 miles to the west of central London, hardly need an introduction. The site was first used for private aviation in 1930, and it was used on occasions by fighters of No.11 Group during the Battle of Britain. Although it was not part of the organizational structure of No. 11 Group, it was part of Fighter Command's contingency plans in 1940 and was nominated as the alternative airfield for the sector airfield of Biggin Hill should it have ever been necessary to evacuate Biggin.

It was occasionally used during the Battle of Britain by detachments of Hurricanes based at nearby Northolt; No. 1 Squadron used it during August and early September, after which No. 229 Squardron used it until the end of the battle. Defiants of No. 264 Squadron, detached to Northolt from their home base at Kirton-in-Lindsey, also operated from Heathrow in a night-fighter role towards the end of the battle. The airfield was later developed to accommodate heavy American bombers but the war came to an end before it was put to use.

After the war the Air Ministry handed it over to civil aviation and it rapidly expanded into one of the world's largest and busiest airports. It can be reached from Junction 4 of the M4, Junction 4A of the A4 and Junction 14 of the M25.

The Runnymede Memorial

Situated on Cooper's Hill at Runnymede, near Windsor, the Runnymede Memorial commemorates more than 20,500 airmen from the RAF and British Commonwealth, and other nations serving with the RAF, who died whilst serving in northern Europe during the Second World War and have no known graves. Her Majesty Queen Elizabeth II unveiled the memorial on 17 October 1953. The site was chosen for its proximity to Heathrow Airport, to retain a link with aviation.

Access is through gates along a central path leading to a three-arched entrance with a stone eagle above, with the names of the missing inscribed on stone in the cloister design. At the far end of the cloister is a large tower with an arched opening, with three sculptured figures above, representing Courage, Justice and Victory. On top of the tower is a turret and a crown. The design of the memorial is such that one of the cloister wings looks out over the valley below towards Heathrow Airport and the other towards Windsor.

Of more than 500 airmen killed during the Battle of Britain, 175 are commemorated on the memorial. However, it does not include the names of those who served in the Fleet Air Arm (commemorated on the Fleed Air Arm Memorial at Lee-on-Solent) or Polish airmen (commemorated on the Polish Air Force Memorial at Northolt).

The Memorial can be found 2 miles to the west of Junction 13 of the M25. It can also be reached by taking the A308 Staines to Windsor road. Driving along the southern side of the River Thames towards Windsor, Runnymede can be seen on the ridge to the left and reached via the A328 just before Old Windsor.

The Runnymede Memorial near Windsor commemorates more than 20,500 airmen who have no known graves.

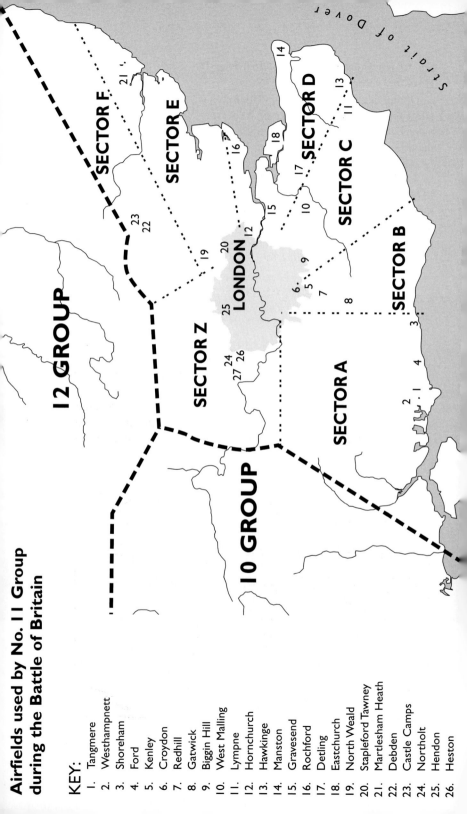

Airfields used by No. 11 Group during the Battle of Britain

KEY:

1. Tangmere
2. Westhampnett
3. Shoreham
4. Ford
5. Kenley
6. Croydon
7. Redhill
8. Gatwick
9. Biggin Hill
10. West Malling
11. Lympne
12. Hornchurch
13. Hawkinge
14. Manston
15. Gravesend
16. Rochford
17. Detling
18. Eastchurch
19. North Weald
20. Stapleford Tawney
21. Martlesham Heath
22. Debden
23. Castle Camps
24. Northolt
25. Hendon
26. Heston

12 GROUP

10 GROUP

SECTOR F

SECTOR E

SECTOR Z

SECTOR D

SECTOR C

SECTOR B

SECTOR A

LONDON

Strait of Dover

CHAPTER TEN

SUMMARY OF THE AIRFIELDS

In this final chapter, I have summarized the airfields in one easy 'at a glance' guide. For a clearer description of locations and directions, you will need to refer to the main chapters. The brief comments I offer for each airfield are very much my own thoughts, but will hopefully be of some use. The intention is to help you decide which of the sites might meet your own particular interest.

Tangmere Sector

Tangmere

Description: Sector airfield.
Location: West Sussex - 3 miles east of Chichester.
Directions: South of the A27. Signposted soon after leaving Chichester on the A27 towards Arundel.
Comments: Well worth a visit, particularly the Tangmere Military Aviation Museum (open daily from February to November) and also the village of Tangmere itself. There is much of interest from the Battle of Britain.
Summary of Squadrons:

Sqn	From	To	Aircraft	Sqn Code
145 Sqn	Start (10/5/40) 9/10/40	31/7/40 End (7/5/41)	Hurricane	SO
43 Sqn	Start (31/5/40) 1/8/40	23/7/40 8/9/40	Hurricane	NQ
601 Sqn	Start (17/6/40) 2/9/40	19/8/40 7/9/40	Hurricane	UF
1 Sqn	Start (23/6/40)	1/8/40	Hurricane	JX
266 Sqn	9/8/40	12/8/40	Spitfire	UO
17 Sqn	19/8/40	2/9/40	Hurricane	YB
607 Sqn	1/9/40	10/10/40	Hurricane	AF
213 Sqn	7/9/40	End (29/11/40)	Hurricane	AK
FIU	Start (18/4/40)	20/8/40	Blenheim	

Westhampnett

Description: Satellite airfield for Tangmere.
Location: West Sussex – 2 miles north-east of Chichester.
Directions: North of the A27. Signposted soon after leaving Chichester on the A27 towards Arundel. Follow signs for Goodwood Aerodrome.
Comments: Worth a visit as there is so much to see, although not relating to the Battle of Britain. Nevertheless, there is flying, motor racing and you can even have a 'flutter' on the horses! Best combined with a visit to Tangmere as the two sites are very close together.
Summary of Squadrons:

Sqn	From	To	Aircraft	Sqn Code
145 Sqn	31/7/40	13/8/40	Hurricane	SO
602 Sqn	14/8/40	End (17/12/40)	Spitfire	LO

Shoreham

Description: Advanced operating airfield for No. 11 Group.
Location: West Sussex – Between Brighton and Worthing.
Directions: On the A27 by Shoreham-on-Sea.
Comments: Used by the FIU and No. 422 Flight. Now a municipal airport.

Ford

Description: Royal Navy airfield used by No. 11 Group.
Location: West Sussex – 2 miles west of Littlehampton.
Directions: From the A27 at Arundel, the site is between Ford and the A259.
Comments: Transferred to No. 11 Group towards the end of the Battle of Britain. Now a prison and used by industry.

Kenley Sector

Kenley

Description: Sector airfield.
Location: Greater London – 5 miles south of Croydon.
Directions: From Croydon, take the A22 towards Caterham. Go through Kenley and turn right at Whyteleafe. Proceed up Whyteleafe Hill and turn right at the top. The airfield is on the right.
Comments: Well worth a visit and a good place to capture the mood of life at an airfield during the Battle of Britain. The airfield is on Kenley

Common and offers a good walk. There is still much to see and a visit to the Tribute to Kenley memorial is recommended, as is St Luke's churchyard at Whyteleafe.

Summary of Squadrons:

Sqn	From	To	Aircraft	Sqn Code
64 Sqn	Start (16/5/40)	18/8/	Spitfire	SH
615 Sqn	Start (20/5/40)	28/8/	Hurricane	KW
616 Sqn	19/8/	2/9/	Spitfire	QJ
253 Sqn	29/8/	End (2/1/41)	Hurricane	SW
66 Sqn	3/9/	10/9/	Spitfire	RB
501 Sqn	10/9/	End (16/12/40)	Hurricane	SD

Croydon

Description: Satellite airfield for Kenley.

Location: Greater London – south-west of Croydon town centre.

Directions: On the A23 Purley Way towards Brighton.

Comments: The airfield has long gone but the Croydon Airport Visitors' Centre is worth a visit for those interested in aviation history as there is so much on offer. Remember, though, that it is only open on the first Sunday of every month. There is nothing else to see relating to the Battle of Britain period, although it is worth stopping at the memorial for a few moments.

Summary of Squadrons:

Sqn	From	To	Aircraft	Sqn Code
111 Sqn	Start (4/6/40)	18/8/40	Hurricane	TM
1 Sqn (RCAF)	Start (3/7/40)	15/8/40	Hurricane	YO
85 Sqn	19/8/40	2/9/40	Hurricane	VY
111 Sqn	3/9/40	7/9/40	Hurricane	TM
72 Sqn	1/9/40	13//9/40	Spitfire	SD
605 Sqn	7/9/40	End (25/2/41)	Hurricane	UP

Redhill

Description: Emergency satellite airfield for Kenley.

Location: Surrey – 3 miles east of Reigate.

Directions: From the A23 heading south, follow the signs for the Aerodrome. From the A25 you need to be to the south of Bletchingley, again following signs for the aerodrome.

Comments: Nothing from the Battle of Britain period but good for watching light aircraft.

Summary of Squadrons:

Sqn	From	To	Aircraft	Sqn Code
600 Sqn	12/9/40	12/10/40	Blenheim	BQ
219 Sqn	12/10/40	End (10/12/40)	Blenheim	FK

Gatwick

Description: Emergency satellite airfield for Kenley.

Location: West Sussex, just north of Crawley.

Directions: M23 Junction 9A.

Comments: Nothing for the Battle of Britain enthusiast but good for plane spotters or going on holiday.

Summary of Squadrons:

Sqn	From	To	Aircraft	Sqn Code
26 Sqn	3/9/40	End (14/7/41)	Lysander	RM
141 Sqn	18/9/40	22/10/40	Defiant	TW

Biggin Hill Sector

Biggin Hill

Description: Sector airfield.

Location: Greater London – 6 miles south-east of Croydon.

Directions: Follow signs from Junction 4 of the M25. Otherwise, follow signs from the A21 and A233 from Bromley towards Westerham.

Comments: Well worth a visit, particularly to St George's Chapel of Remembrance. The chapel is open daily to visitors.

Summary of Squadrons:

Sqn	From	To	Aircraft	Sqn Code
32 Sqn	Start (4/6/40)	27/8/40	Hurricane	KT
610 Sqn	Start (2/7/40)	12/9/40	Spitfire	DW
79 Sqn	27/8/40	7/9/40	Hurricane	AL
72 Sqn	31/8/40 14/9/40	1/9/40 12/10/40	Spitfire	SD
141 Sqn	13/9/40	18/9/40	Defiant	TW
92 Sqn	8/9/40	End (9/1/41)	Spitfire	GR
74 Sqn	15/10/40	End (20/2/41)	Spitfire	ZP

West Malling

Description: Used as a forward operating airfield for Biggin Hill and also as a satellite airfield for Kenley.
Location: Kent. – 7 miles north-west of Maidstone.
Directions: From Junction 4 of the M20 take the A228 towards Tonbridge. The site is at King's Hill.
Comments: Although the airfield has gone and new buildings have appeared, every attempt has been made to preserve the history. The old air traffic control tower and the memorial are worth a visit if you are in the area.
Summary of Squadrons:

Sqn	From	To	Aircraft	Sqn Code
26 Sqn	Start (8/6/40)	3/9/40	Lysander	RM
141 Sqn	12/7/40	21/7/40	Defiant	TW
66 Sqn	30/10/40	End (7/11/40)	Spitfire	RB/LZ

Lympne

Description: Forward operating airfield for No. 11 Group.
Location: Kent – 7 miles west of Folkestone.
Directions: On the B2067 towards Port Lympne.
Comments: Now Lympne Industrial Park and nothing left of particular interest.

Hornchurch Sector

Hornchurch

Description: Sector airfield.
Location: Greater London – 3 miles north of Rainham.
Directions: From the A1306 take the A125 Rainham to Hornchurch road and follow signs to the Hornchurch Country Park.
Comments: Worth a visit. The site is now the Hornchurch Country Park and every effort has been made in the local area to preserve the history of this famous airfield. As a warning, the traffic can get very busy in the vicinity if you are heading towards Hornchurch from the north or west. I suggest you approach from the east.

Summary of Squadrons:

Sqn	From	To	Aircraft	Sqn Code
65 Sqn	Start (5/6/40)	28/8/40	Spitfire	FZ
74 Sqn	Start (25/6/40)	14/8/40	Spitfire	JH
54 Sqn	24/7/40 8/8/40	28/7/40 3/9/40	Spitfire	KL
41 Sqn	26/7/40 3/9/40	8/8/40 End (23/2/41)	Spitfire	EB
266 Sqn	14/8/40	21/8/40	Spitfire	UO
264 Sqn	22/8/40	28/8/40	Defiant	PS
600 Sqn	22/8/40	12/9/40	Blenheim	BQ
603 Sqn	27/8/40	End (3/12/40)	Spitfire	XT
222 Sqn	29/8/40	End (11/11/40)	Spitfire	ZD

Hawkinge

Description: Forward operating airfield for No. 11 Group.

Location: Kent – north of Folkestone.

Directions: From the A20 take the A260 towards Canterbury and follow the signs to the Kent Battle of Britain Museum.

Comments: This is a must for the Battle of Britain enthusiast as there is much to see. Combine a visit to the Kent Battle of Britain Museum with a stroll around the edge of the airfield. The museum is open Tuesday to Sunday between Easter and the end of September but remember that photography or recording of any kind is prohibited. Make sure that whilst you are in the area you visit the National Memorial to the Battle of Britain at Capel-le-Ferne. It really is a most beautiful setting.

Summary of Squadrons:

Squadron (home base in brackets)	Aircraft	Sqn Code
79 Sqn (Biggin Hill)	Hurricane	AL
141 Sqn (West Malling)	Defiant	TW
32 Sqn (Biggin Hill)	Hurricane	KT
501 Sqn (Gravesend)	Hurricane	SD
615 Sqn (Kenley)	Hurricane	KW
111 Sqn (Croydon)	Hurricane	TM
72 Sqn (Croydon)	Spitfire	RN
610 Sqn (Biggin Hill)	Spitfire	DW

Manston

Description: Forward operating airfield for No. 11 Group.

Location: Kent – on the Isle of Thanet, just west of Ramsgate.

Directions: Follow the signs to Kent International Airport. From the A259 towards Ramsgate, take the B2190 and follow the signs for the Spitfire and Hurricane Memorial Building.

Comments: Well worth a visit even though the Isle of Thanet is a bit out of the way. I was very impressed with the Spitfire and Hurricane Memorial Building, as there is so much to see relating to the Battle of Britain. The museum is open throughout the year. Whilst there you should also visit the RAF Manston History Museum.

Summary of Squadrons:

Sqn	From	To	Aircraft	Sqn Code
600 Sqn	Start (20/6/40)	22/8/40	Blenheim	BQ

Gravesend

Description: Satellite airfield for Biggin Hill.

Location: Kent – 7 miles east of the Dartford Tunnel on the southern side of the Thames.

Directions: From the M25 follow the A2 towards Rochester. To the east of Gravesend take the road to the village of Thong and continue to the site of the Leisure Complex.

Comments: This is one for the most enthusiastic enthusiast as there is nothing left except a plaque in the Leisure Centre, which remembers the fifteen pilots killed whilst serving at the airfield during the Battle of Britain.

Summary of Squadrons:

Sqn	From	To	Aircraft	Sqn Code
604 Sqn	Start (3/7/40)	26/7/40	Blenheim	NG
501 Sqn	25/7/40	10/9/40	Hurricane	SD
66 Sqn	11/9/40	30/10/40	Spitfire	RB/LZ
421 Flight	7/10/40	30/10/40	Hurricane Spitfire	L-Z

Rochford

Description: Satellite airfield for Hornchurch and North Weald.

Location: Essex – just to the north of Southend-on-Sea.

Directions: Follow the signs for Southend Airport. From the A127 at

Southend-on-Sea take the A1159 towards Rochford.

Comments: Now Southend Airport and nothing for the Battle of Britain enthusiast. Otherwise, a good day out at the seaside and a chance to see some aircraft.

Summary of Squadrons:

Sqn	From	To	Aircraft	Sqn Code
54 Sqn	Start (25/6/40)	24/7/40	Spitfire	KL
264 Sqn	27/8/40 29/10/40	28/8/40 End (27/11/40)	Defiant	PS

Detling

Description: Coastal Command airfield used by No. 11 Group.

Location: Kent – just north-east of Maidstone.

Directions: From Junction 7 of the M20 take the A249 towards Sheerness.

Comments: Now Kent County Showground, but some reminders of the airfield exist.

Eastchurch

Description: Coastal Command airfield used by No. 11 Group.

Location: Kent – on the Isle of Sheppey.

Directions: Take the B2231 toward Leysdown and follow signs for the prisons.

Comments: Now Standford Hill prison but an important early site of aviation.

North Weald Sector

North weald

Description: Sector airfield.

Location: Essex – just south-east of Harlow.

Directions: Follow the signs from the M11 along the A414 towards Chelmsford.

Comments: Well worth a visit. The airfield has survived, as have some of the buildings, and there is much going on at the weekends. Whilst there make sure you visit the North Weald Airfield Museum, which is open every weekend from Easter to October.

Summary of Squadrons:

Sqn	From	To	Aircraft	Sqn Code
56 Sqn	Start (4/6/40)	1//9/40	Hurricane	LR/US
151 Sqn	Start (20/5/40)	29/8/40	Hurricane	DZ
249 Sqn	1/9/40	End (1/5/41)	Hurricane	GN
25 Sqn	1/9/40	8/10/40	Blenheim	ZK
257 Sqn	8/10/40	End (7/11/40)	Hurricane	DT

Stapleford Tawney

Description: Satellite airfield for North Weald.
Location: Essex – Between Chigwell and Chipping Ongar.
Directions: On the south side of the M25, the airfield is on the A113 just west of the B175 towards Romford.
Comments: Although the airfield has survived, there is nothing for the Battle of Britain enthusiast. Now Stapleford Flying Club and good for pleasure flights or private flying.
Summary of Squadrons:

Sqn	From	To	Aircraft	Sqn Code
151 Sqn	29/8/40	1/9/40	Hurricane	DZ
46 Sqn	1/9/40	End (8/11/40)	Hurricane	PO

Martlesham Heath

Description: Forward operating airfield for No. 11 Group, mainly used by Debden.
Location: Suffolk – 3 miles east of Ipswich.
Directions: From the A14 towards Felixstowe, take the A12 north to Martlesham Heath.
Comments: Worth a visit. Although this site is some considerable distance from the other airfields of No. 11 Group, there is still much to see, even though the airfield has gone. In particular, the Control Tower Museum and wooded area behind it is worth a visit. Remember that the museum is only open on Sunday afternoons between Easter and October. There are also several old buildings that have survived. Overall, I was very pleasantly surprised.

Summary of Squadrons:

Sqn	From	To	Aircraft	Sqn Code
25 Sqn	Start (19/6/40)	1/9/40	Blenheim	ZK
257 Sqn	5/9/40	8/10/40	Hurricane	DT
17 Sqn	8/10/40	End (28/2/41)	Hurricane	YB

Debden Sector

Debden

Description: Sector airfield.

Location: Essex – just south-east of Saffron Walden.

Directions: From Saffron Walden take the B184 towards Thaxted, which passes the eastern boundary of the airfield just before the turn-off for Debden village.

Comments: You would have to be keen to pursue this one. The site is now Carver Barracks and, although the airfield remains, there is no access to the site without prior permission.

Summary of Squadrons:

Sqn	From	To	Aircraft	Sqn Code
17 Sqn	Start (19/6/40) 2/9/40	19/8/40 8/10/40	Hurricane	YB
85 Sqn	Start (22/5/40) 3/9/40	19/8/40 5/9/40	Hurricane	VY
257 Sqn	15/8/40	5/9/40	Hurricane	DT
111 Sqn	19/8/40	3/9/40	Hurricane	TM
601 Sqn	19/8/40	2/9/40	Hurricane	UF
25 Sqn	8/10/40	End (27/11/40)	Blenheim Beaufighter	ZK

Castle Camps

Description: Satellite airfield for Debden.

Location: Essex – remote, about 10 miles north-east of Debden and 3 miles south-west of Haverhill.

Directions: South of the A1307 at Mill Hill, between Linton and Haverhill. You then need to get yourself on the narrow country road from Castle Camps towards Helions Bumpstead.

Comments: This is definitely one for the most enthusiastic enthusiast. There is nothing much there except farmers' fields, although the village of Castle Camps does have a memorial.

Summary of Squadrons:

Sqn	From	To	Aircraft	Sqn Code
85 Sqn	3/9/40	5/9/40	Hurricane	VY
73 Sqn	5/9/40	End (13/11/40)	Hurricane	TP

Northolt Sector

Northolt

Description: Sector airfield.

Location: Greater London – 15 miles west of central London on the A40 Western Avenue.

Directions: From the end of the M40, continue along the A40 towards London.

Comments: This is the only airfield still in use by the RAF. There is no access to the site without prior permission. If in the area it is worth visiting the Polish Air Force Memorial, which is just outside the airfield's south-eastern boundary. Also worth a visit is the Runnymede Memorial, near Windsor.

Summary of Squadrons:

Sqn	From	To	Aircraft	Sqn Code
257 Sqn	Start (4/7/40)	14/8/40	Hurricane	DT
1 Sqn	Start (18/6/40) 1/8/40	23/7/40 9/9/40	Hurricane	JX
43 Sqn	23/7/40	1/8/40	Hurricane	NQ
303 Sqn	22/7/40	11/10/40	Hurricane	RF
1 Sqn (RCAF)	16/8/40	10/10/40	Hurricane	YO
229 Sqn	9/9/40	End (15/12/40)	Hurricane	RE
615 Sqn	10/10/40	End (17/12/40)	Hurricane	KW
302 Sqn	11/10/40	End (23/11/40)	Hurricane	WX

Hendon

Description: Operating Airfield.

Location: Greater London – 10 miles north of central London near Junction 1 of the M1.

Directions: From Junction 1 of the M1, or from the A1 or A41 heading south into London, follow the signs for the RAF Museum. Consider taking the Underground, on the Northern Line to Colindale and then a short walk.

Comments: The RAF Museum is a must for the Battle of Britain enthusiast.

Summary of Squadrons:

Sqn	From	To	Aircraft	Sqn Code
504 Sqn	5/9/40	26/9/40	Hurricane	TM

Heston

Description: Satellite airfield for Northolt.

Location: Greater London – 20 miles west of central London.

Directions: M4 heading west just before Junction 3.

Comments: Used by No. 1 PRU during the Battle of Britain. The M4 passes through the site and there is nothing left of interest for the Battle of Britain.

Heathrow

Description: Operating Airfield.

Location: Greater London – 20 miles west of central London.

Directions: M4 Junction 4 or Junction 4A of the A4. Otherwise Junction 14 of the M25.

Comments: Used occasionally by squadrons based at Northolt. Now Heathrow Airport. Good for plane spotters and holidays!

A SUMMARY OF EVENTS OF THE BATTLE OF BRITAIN

Below is a simplified table covering the chronology of events of the Battle of Britain. The number of phases and the dates of each phase, vary according to source, and the dates used in this appendix should only be taken as a guide.

Phase	Dates of Summary Period and Weather Condition	Summary of Main Activity	Summary of Losses (approximate as sources vary)	
One			LUFTWAFFE	RAF
	10 – 24 July Weather generally unsettled with much cloud and occasional rain showers.	Air fighting over the Channel convoy 'Bread' on 10 July marked the official start of the Battle of Britain. Attacks against shipping in the Channel and off the south and east coast. Occasional attacks against ports and towns.	90–100	50
	25 July – 5 August Weather improved during the period and, apart from 26–27 July, was fine throughout.	Increased air activity on fine weather days. Attacks against shipping continued. Channel convoys suspended by day.	80–90	20–25
	6 – 10 August Weather generally unsettled, but bright periods on 8 August.	Little activity on poor days but heavy attacks on 8 August due to improved weather, which resulted in the heaviest air activity to date.	35–40	25
Two				
	11 – 12 August Good weather.	After two quiet days, air fighting intensified with air attacks against shipping and ports.	65–70	50–55
	13 August Good weather.	German high command launched *Adlertag* and changed its priority to attacking the vital airfields of Fighter Command.	40–50	10–15

14 – 19 August Good weather.	Heavy raids on several RAF airfields and radar sites. Heaviest fighting to date on 15 August with the *Luftwaffe* flying over 2,000 sorties and the RAF about 1,000. Both sides suffered the highest daily losses to date (55–75 *Luftwaffe*, (depending on source and 34 RAF). Heavy raids and air fighting on 18 August.	210–220	90–95
20 – 23 August Weather unsettled. Cloudy, windy and rain showers.	Limited air activity due to weather, although there were raids across the country on 22 August.	25–30	5–10
24 August – 6 September Weather generally good throughout.	Large increase in air activity. Continuous period of heavy raids against Fighter Command's airfields. Night attacks against factories, towns and cities.	370–400	280–290
Three			
7 – 15 September Weather generally good throughout.	*Luftwaffe* concentrated on bombing London, which gave Fighter Command a vital rest following a sustained period of raids against its airfields – arguably the turning point of the battle. Main targets were Thameshaven and London Docks. Start of night-bombing offensive against London – the Blitz. The largest daylight raids took place on 15 September and Fighter Command was stretched to its limit. The *Luftwaffe*, in particular, suffered heavy losses (approximate 60 aircraft) and the day has since become celebrated as 'Battle of Britain Day'.	200	120
16 – 22 September Weather unsettled with large amounts of cloud and several rain showers.	Limited air activity by day due to unsettled weather. Continuous night attacks against London.	40–50	25

	23 – 30 September Good weather.	Further attacks against London and towns, cities and factories across the rest of the country. Heavy raids, in particular, on 27 September with high losses on both sides. Night offensive against London and other towns and cities continued.	160–170	100
Four				
	1 – 31 October Weather for the first two days was good. It then changed and remained unsettled for most of the month, with much cloud and a mix of showers and bright periods.	Final phase of the battle. The *Luftwaffe* used smaller formations of bombers by day and also fighters carrying bombs in penetrating raids against airfields and factories. The main *Luftwaffe* air activity was by night against London and other towns and cities. Heaviest night raids on London were on 14-15 October.	300–320	140–150
		TOTAL LOSSES	1,615–1,740	915–960

APPENDIX II

No. 11 GROUP
ORDER OF BATTLE

15 July 1940

SECTOR	AIRFIELD	SQUADRON
Tangmere	Tangmere Shoreham	43 (H), 145 (H), 601 (H) FIU (B)
Kenley	Kenley Croydon	64 (S), 615 (H) 111 (H), 1(RCAF) (H)
Biggin Hill	Biggin Hill West Malling Gravesend	32 (H), 610 (S) 141 (D) 604 (B)
Hornchurch	Hornchurch Rochford Manston	65 (S), 74 (S) 54 (S) 600 (B)
North Weald	North Weald Martlesham Heath	56 (H), 151 (H) 25 (B)
Debden	Debden	17 (H), 85 (H)
Northolt	Northolt	1 (H), 257 (H)

18 August 1940

SECTOR	AIRFIELD	SQUADRON
Tangmere	Tangmere Westhampnett Shoreham	43 (H), 601 (H) 602 (S) FIU (B)
Kenley	Kenley Croydon	64 (S), 615 (H) 111 (H)
Biggin Hill	Biggin Hill Gravesend	32 (H), 610 (S) 501 (H)
Hornchurch	Hornchurch Manston	54 (S), 65 (S), 266 (S) 600 (B)
North Weald	North Weald Martlesham Heath	56 (H), 151 (H) 25 (B)
Debden	Debden	17 (H), 85 (H), 257 (H)
Northolt	Northolt	1 (H), 303 (H), 1(RCAF) (H)

15 September 1940

SECTOR	AIRFIELD	SQUADRON
Tangmere	Tangmere Westhampnett Ford Shoreham	213 (H), 607 (H) 602 (S) 23 (B) FIU (B)
Kenley	Kenley Croydon Redhill	253 (H), 501 (H) 605 (H) 600 (B)
Biggin Hill	Biggin Hill Gravesend	72 (S), 92 (S), 141 (D) 66 (S)
Hornchurch	Hornchurch	41 (S), 222 (S), 603 (S)
North Weald	North Weald Stapleford Tawney Martlesham Heath	249 (H), 25 (B) 46 (H) 257 (H)
Debden	Debden Castle Camps	17 (H) 73 (H)
Northolt	Northolt Hendon	229 (H), 303 (H), 1(RCAF) (H) 504 (H)

31 October 1940

SECTOR	AIRFIELD	SQUADRON
Tangmere	Tangmere Westhampnett Ford Shoreham	145 (H), 213 (H) 602 (S) 23 (B) FIU (B/B), 422 Flt (H)
Kenley	Kenley Croydon Redhill	253 (H), 501 (H) 605 (H) 219 (B)
Biggin Hill	Biggin Hill West Malling	74 (S), 92 (S) 66 (S), 421 Flt (H)
Hornchurch	Hornchurch Rochford	41 (S), 222 (S), 603 (S) 264 (D)
North Weald	North Weald Stapleford Tawney Martlesham Heath	249 (H), 257 (H) 46 (H) 17 (H)
Debden	Debden Castle Camps	25 (B/B) 73 (H)
Northolt	Northolt	229 (H), 302 (H), 615 (H)

Key: H = Hurricane
S = Spitfire
B = Blenheim
B/B = Blenheim/Beaufighter
D = Defiant

BIBLIOGRAPHY

Air Ministry combat reports (various)

Air Ministry log books (various)

Air Ministry Squadron History Forms F540 (various)

Air Ministry Squadron History Forms F541 (various)

Ashworth, Chris, *Action Stations 9* (Patrick Stephens Ltd, 1985)

Bowyer, Chaz, *Hurricane at War* (Ian Allan, 1974)

Bowyer, Chaz, *History of the RAF* (Hamlyn, 1979)

Bowyer, Michael J.F., *Action Stations 1* (Patrick Stephens Ltd, 1979)

Cluett, Douglas, Bogle, Joanna and Learmonth, Bob, *Croydon Airport and the Battle for Britain* (Sutton Libraries, 1984)

Cossey, Bob, *Tigers – The Story of No. 74 Squadron RAF* (Arms & Armour Press, 1992)

Cull, Brian, *249 at War* (Grub Street, 1997)

Deighton, Len, *Battle of Britain* (Book Club Associates, 1980)

Delve, Ken, *Source Book of the RAF* (Airlife, 1994)

Gelb, Norman, *Scramble. A Narrative History* (Michael Joseph Ltd, 1986)

Gretzyngier, Robert, *Poles in Defence of Britain* (Grub Street, 2001)

Halfpenny, Bruce Barrymore, *Action Stations 8* (Patrick Stephens Ltd, 1984)

Halley, James J., *Squadrons of the RAF and Commonwealth* (Air Britain, 1988)

Hough, Richard and Richards, Denis, *The Battle of Britain* (Guild Publishing, 1990)

Jacobs, Peter, *Hawker Hurricane* (Crowood Press Ltd, 1998)

James, T.C.G., *The Battle of Britain* (Frank Cass Publishers, 2000)

Johnson, Air Vice-Marshal 'Johnnie' and Lucas, Wing Commander 'Laddie', *Winged Victory* (Stanley Paul, 1995)

Kaplan, Richard, and Collier, Richard, *The Few* (Blandford, 1989)

Leeson, Frank M., *The Hornet Strikes – The Story of No. 213 Squadron RAF* (Air Britain, 1998)

Mason, Francis K., *The Hawker Hurricane* (Aston, 1987)

Mason, Tim, *British Flight Testing – Martlesham Heath 1920–39* (Putnam Aeronatical Books, 1993)

Murray, Williamson, *Strategy for Defeat – The Luftwaffe 1933–45* (Eagle Editions, 2000)

Price, Dr Alfred, *Battle of Britain Day* (Sidgwick & Jackson, 1990)

Price, Alfred, *The Hardest Day* (Arms & Armour Press, 1988)

RAF Museum, *Against the Odds – The Battle of Britain Experience* (Battle of Britain Ltd, 1990)

Ramsey, Winston G., (ed), *Battle of Britain, Then and Now* (Battle of Britain Prints Int, 1989)

Rawlings, John D.R., *Fighter Squadrons of the RAF and Their Aircraft* (MacDonald & Co, 1969)

Rawlings, John, *History of the RAF* (Temple Press, 1984)

Robinson, Anthony, *RAF Squadrons in the Battle of Britain* (Arms & Armour Press, 1987)

Rowland, P.G., *'Brave and Calm, Chaps' – The Story of Squadron Leader H.T.Gilbert DFC* (Mortons of Horncastle, 1990)

Shores, Christopher, and Williams, Clive, *Aces High* (Grub Street, 1994)

Shores, Christopher, *Aces High Volume 2* (Grub Street, 1999)

Stones, Donald, *Dimsie* (Wingham Press, 1991)

Tavender, I.T., *The Distinguished Flying Medal* (J B Hayward & Son, 1990)

Terraine, John, *The Right of the Line* (Hodder & Stoughton, 1985)

Townsend Bickers, Richard, *The Battle of Britain* (Salamander Books, 1990)

Townsend Bickers, Richard, *Ginger Lacey – Fighter Pilot*, revised edition, (Robert Hale, 1997)

Wynn, Humphrey (ed), *Fighter Pilot – A Self Portrait by George Barclay* (Crecy Books, 1994)

Wynn, Kenneth G., *Men of the Battle of Britain* (Gliddon Books, 1989)